"These clinically rich and empathic studies of those depending on the cold comforts afforded by dismissing attachment to protect them against the fear of social engagement provide vivid insights into the predicament they face, especially when they find themselves on the threshold of therapy. Engaging the reader with this often hard-to-reach group they offer a valuable theoretical and practical resource for those helping them come out of the cold."
Christopher Clulow, PhD, Senior Fellow, the Tavistock Institute of Medical Psychology, London.

"Although many people inflict horrific cruelty upon their partners, the vast majority cause pain as a result of emotional unavailability, fuelled by avoidant attachment structures. In this superb book, Linda Cundy provides us with four remarkable master classes in the understanding of this often invisible, yet devastating, form of interpersonal interaction. Drawing upon extensive clinical experience and empirical research, the authors offer us a truly comprehensive textbook which will enlighten all of our clinical practices."
Professor Brett Kahr, Senior Fellow at Tavistock Relationships, Tavistock Institute of Medical Psychology, London, Senior Clinical Research Fellow at the Centre for Child Mental Health, London, Consultant in Psychology at The Bowlby Centre, Trustee of the Freud Museum London.

ATTACHMENT AND THE DEFENCE AGAINST INTIMACY

This book combines attachment theory and research with clinical experience to provide practitioners with tools for engaging with individuals who are indifferent, avoidant, highly defensive, and who struggle to make and maintain intimate connections with others. Composed of four papers presented at a Wimbledon Guild conference in 2017, this text examines the origins of avoidant attachment patterns in early life, describes research tools that offer a more refined understanding of this insecure attachment pattern, explores the internal object worlds of "dismissing" adults, and considers the impact on couple relationships when one or both partners avoid intimacy or dependency.

Each chapter contains case studies with children and families, adolescents, adults, and couples that acknowledge the challenges of engaging with these "shut down" individuals, with authors sharing what they have learned from their patients about what is needed for effective psychotherapy. It is an accessible book full of clinical richness and insight that will be invaluable to practitioners who are interested in deepening their understanding and clinical skills from an attachment perspective.

Linda Cundy is an attachment-based psychoanalytic psychotherapist and supervisor in private practice in North London. She is also an independent trainer and an author.

ATTACHMENT AND THE DEFENCE AGAINST INTIMACY

Understanding and Working with Avoidant Attachment, Self-Hatred, and Shame

Edited by
Linda Cundy

First published 2019
by Routledge
2 Park Square, Milton Park, Abingdon, Oxon OX14 4RN

and by Routledge
711 Third Avenue, New York, NY 10017

Routledge is an imprint of the Taylor & Francis Group, an informa business

© 2019 selection and editorial matter, Linda Cundy; individual chapters, the contributors

The right of Linda Cundy to be identified as the author of the editorial matter, and of the authors for their individual chapters, has been asserted in accordance with sections 77 and 78 of the Copyright, Designs and Patents Act 1988.

All rights reserved. No part of this book may be reprinted or reproduced or utilised in any form or by any electronic, mechanical, or other means, now known or hereafter invented, including photocopying and recording, or in any information storage or retrieval system, without permission in writing from the publishers.

Trademark notice: Product or corporate names may be trademarks or registered trademarks, and are used only for identification and explanation without intent to infringe.

British Library Cataloguing-in-Publication Data
A catalogue record for this book is available from the British Library

Library of Congress Cataloging-in-Publication Data
A catalog record has been requested for this book

ISBN: 978-1-138-61497-0 (hbk)
ISBN: 978-1-138-33045-0 (pbk)
ISBN: 978-0-429-44786-0 (ebk)

Typeset in Palatino
by Wearset Ltd, Boldon, Tyne and Wear

CONTENTS

ACKNOWLEDGEMENTS ix

ABOUT THE EDITOR AND CONTRIBUTORS xi

INTRODUCTION xiv
Maggie Turp

CHAPTER ONE
Avoiding avoidance: neglecting emotional neglect and deactivated relationship styles 1
Graham Music

CHAPTER TWO
Not trying to avoid the bridge: avoidant attachment from research to clinical practice 23
Andrea Oskis

CHAPTER THREE
Avoidant people in relationships: why would they bother? How do partners fare? 37
Anne Power

CHAPTER FOUR
Masters in the art of defence: shame and defences against intimacy   69
Linda Cundy

INDEX   109

ACKNOWLEDGEMENTS

Attachment and the Defence Against Intimacy: Understanding and Working with Avoidant Attachment, Self-Hatred, and Shame is the monograph of the 2017 Wimbledon Guild conference and is the second of a series, following *Anxiously Attached: Understanding and Working with Preoccupied Attachment*, published by Karnac (2017).

The Wimbledon Guild has a long tradition of promoting attachment theory, providing one-day seminars, conferences, and training courses. When I taught the first of these in 2000 I had the good fortune to meet Regina King who was, by then, retired from her role at the Guild. Gina had trained as a social worker at the Tavistock Institute where she worked under John Bowlby, and I am sure she would be delighted that his legacy lives on through these conferences and training events. I thank the Chief Executive Officer of the Wimbledon Guild, Wendy Pridmore, and Georgina Hoare, Head of Talking Therapies, for their part in continuing this long relationship; thanks, also, to Mark Morgenroth who helped to organise this successful conference.

On the day, we were fortunate to have an excellent, well-balanced programme of presentations. I am most grateful to Andrea Oskis, Anne Power, and Graham Music for their rich, engaging, and moving talks, and for taking the time to write them up for this book. John Bowlby believed that therapeutic practice should be informed by sound empirical knowledge as well as clinical experience. Contributors to this book draw upon many years of expertise in their own fields to demonstrate how attachment research underpins practice in the consulting room. We have here four complementary chapters that do justice to a group of clients – children, adults, and couples – who are often overlooked, offering insight into the difficulties they so often experience in their relationships with other people and with themselves. Speaking at the Tavistock Clinic Social Work Continuation Group at the end of a long and distinguished career, Bowlby acknowledged that he had been accused of focusing too much on external reality at the expense of the internal world. With no trace of regret he replied, "So be it", explaining that he had dedicated most of his working life to redressing what he perceived to be an imbalance, with psychoanalysis at that time over-privileging unconscious fantasy. Contemporary attachment theory and practice attends to both, the interplay of environmental context, real lived experience, and relational dynamics as they are influenced by, and contribute to, unconscious processes and fantasy. These four chapters reflect this nuanced complexity.

I express my gratitude to Maggie Turp, who chaired the conference with her characteristic light touch, creating an inclusive, friendly atmosphere appropriate to the occasion. Thanks also to Maggie for contributing the Introduction to this collection of papers and for her guidance and encouragement as I prepared my own chapter and edited the book.

Finally, my thanks go to staff at Routledge who provided support and advice throughout the process of preparing this monograph.

ABOUT THE EDITOR AND CONTRIBUTORS

Linda Cundy is an attachment-based psychoanalytic psychotherapist and supervisor in private practice, and a trainer specialising in attachment. She has taught on a number of psychotherapy training courses including at the School of Psychotherapy and Counselling Psychology, Regent's College (now Regent's University), The Bowlby Centre, and the Association for Group and Individual Psychotherapy (AGIP). She developed and instituted the Postgraduate Diploma in Attachment-Based Therapy, a programme that has run successfully at the Wimbledon Guild for the past four years. Linda's publications include several journal papers, a single authored book, *Love in the Age of the Internet: Attachment in the Digital Era* (Karnac, 2015), and an edited monograph, *Anxiously Attached: Understanding and Working with Preoccupied Attachment* (Karnac, 2017). She continues to run one-day training events on a freelance basis and intends in the future to devote more time to her writing and consultancy work.

Graham Music (PhD) is Consultant Child and Adolescent Psychotherapist at the Tavistock and Portman Clinics, and an adult psychotherapist in private practice. His publications include *Nurturing Natures* (2016), *Affect and Emotion* (2001), and *The Good Life* (2014). He has a particular interest in exploring the interface between developmental findings and clinical work. Formerly Associate Clinical Director of the Tavistock's child and family department, he has managed a range of services working with the aftermath of child maltreatment and neglect and organised many community based psychotherapy services. He currently works clinically with forensic cases at The Portman Clinic. He teaches, lectures, and supervises on a range of trainings in Britain and abroad.

Andrea Oskis is a Senior Lecturer in Psychology at Middlesex University, London. Her teaching and research expertise is primarily developmental, with subfields in psychophysiology and clinical health psychology. She specialises in interview assessments of attachment style, parenting, and early experiences of care and abuse. Her research is conducted as part of the Centre for Abuse and Trauma Studies (CATS), based at Middlesex University. She is also an attachment-based psychoanalytic psychotherapist in private practice and a member of the Bowlby Centre.

Anne Power qualified at The Bowlby Centre in attachment-based psychoanalytic psychotherapy after counselling and group-work training She did an MA in supervision at the Westminster Pastoral Foundation, Roehampton and then couple training with Relate. She is a visiting lecturer at Regent's University, London and has a private practice in London. She has written papers on attachment, supervision, and on work with couples, and she leads workshops on all these subjects. Her book, *Forced Endings in Psychotherapy* (Routledge, 2016), explores the process of closing a practice for retirement or for other reasons. Her current research looks at couple relationships in different cultural contexts and she is interviewing couples who came together through random romance, arranged marriage, or via dating services, whether online or actual.

Maggie Turp, C. Psychol, HCPC is a psychoanalytic psychotherapist and supervisor in private practice, and a chartered psychologist. Her academic career has included lectureships at the University of Reading and Birkbeck College, London. Since retiring from mainstream academic life, Maggie has lectured widely and is an occasional visiting lecturer at the Tavistock and Portman Trust. She is a member of the editorial boards of the journals *Psychodynamic Practice* and *Infant Observation*. Her publications include journal papers, book chapters and two books, *Psychosomatic Health: The Body and the Word* (Palgrave, 2001) and

Hidden Self-Harm: Narratives from Psychotherapy (Jessica Kingsley, 2003). An area of current interest is the integration of narrative, attachment-based, and psychodynamic approaches within psychotherapy. She is also working on a novel *The Limits of the Land*, which explores the physical and psychological challenge of climate change. She welcomes correspondence at maggieturp@googlemail.com

INTRODUCTION

Maggie Turp

This book is the sister volume to *Anxiously Attached: Understanding and Working with Preoccupied Attachment*, published by Karnac in 2017. Both books emerged from conferences organised at the Wimbledon Guild with the involvement of the editor, Linda Cundy – events that brought together attachment-based practitioners, object relations practitioners, researchers in the field of attachment, and a large and actively engaged audience of students, researchers, and clinicians.

While the preoccupied individual is "filled with anxious fretting and grievance" (Cundy 2017) in regard to both his or her external attachment figures and their internal representations, the avoidant individual is apparently insouciant, even indifferent, cocooned as he or she is in a shell of pseudo-self-sufficiency. The defensive nature of the avoidant style and the various ways in which it manifests is explored by each of the authors in turn. The common element behind the various manifestations is posited as "a profound belief that you have to stand on your own two feet, that seeking help is a form of weakness, [and] that strong emotions should be avoided, particularly upsetting negative ones" (Music, Chapter 1, p. 1).

This belief finds expression in the paradoxical situation of an individual coming into therapy ostensibly to find help but without any expectation that help will be forthcoming, or is even a possibility. As

Cundy makes clear in Chapter 4, dismissive individuals are more likely to "consult an expert" (p. 93) than to seek therapy. A significant proportion of those who come into therapy are "sent", most often by a concerned parent or frustrated spouse. Nevertheless, there are some who find a way to take the step voluntarily – a major achievement in itself considering their fundamental belief in self-sufficiency – but once in the consulting room find it difficult to become truly engaged. Cundy describes a common pattern of compliance, an absence of emotional engagement or interest in the therapist as a person, and a desire above all to get through a session and be "no trouble at all" (p. 93).

We learn as we read on of the myriad ways in which this situation is played out and the issues it raises in the countertransference. These are patients who are often experienced as unrewarding to work with and who easily slip out of mind. The authors' generous sharing of their struggles to both maintain their own aliveness and bring the patient alive is a particular strength of the book. Together with the lucid and moving accounts of clinical work included in each chapter, reflections on countertransference responses place the reader in the room with practitioner and patient, helping each of us find our own live response to the all too well-disguised need and distress lurking behind the defensive façade.

Graham Music's practice is primarily in the field of child psychotherapy and his case study material eloquently illustrates how babies and toddlers who are ignored and neglected develop into children who "act as if they don't need us or anyone, making us feel useless" (p. 7). In Chapter 1, Music describes how the initial neglect by caregivers can resonate down the years, resulting in double and even triple deprivation. The feelings stirred up in the countertransference – the dread, the lethargy and the "deadening thud inside" (p. 3) – carry with them the risk of further emotional neglect on the part of practitioners, teachers, and foster parents, resulting in the eventual emergence into adulthood of an individual who on no account looks to others for help, convinced as he or she is that seeking help or emotional support will only open the door to further experiences of frustration and disappointment. The negative implications for intimacy are clear.

Music illustrates his engagement with these issues in moving accounts of his clinical work with "Troy" and "Lucy". He also refers to his own experience of being sent to boarding school and the links between experiences such as these, where the needy parts of the personality have to be denied, and the wider culture, in particular the British "stiff upper lip" personality style. Chapter 1 draws on a wide range of references, moving easily between object relations theory, particularly the work of the Independent School, findings from the Strange Situation Test, psychoanalytically informed infancy research, and neuroscience.

In Chapter 2, by Andrea Oskis, we have the advantage of considering avoidant phenomena from both a research and a practice point of view. Drawing on both sources, Oskis presents the reader with a clear and detailed exposition of the wide range of presentations found in "avoidant" clients, including anger and a tendency to withdraw, as well as self-sufficiency, combined with a scale of intensity. This offers a helpful backdrop to the clinical vignettes included by each of the authors as well as to Oskis's own examples.

At the previous conference on preoccupied attachment and in the book emerging from it, Steve Farnfield presented findings from the Adult Attachment Interview (AAI). In Chapter 2, Oskis offers a valuable opportunity to compare and contrast the two interview procedures. Oskis's research findings are grounded, on the one hand, in her clinical work and, on the other, in Attachment Style Interview (ASI) material. She sets out clearly what is explored by the AAI and the ASI respectively: "Whereas the AAI focuses on the 'way' of the description, i.e. the way the individual describes their relationships with their parents (for example with idealisation or derogation), the ASI focuses on the 'what', i.e. what is described" (p. 25). Hence, there is less emphasis in the ASI on the inner world of the interviewee and more on his or her outer world. Discussing links to clinical practice, Oskis describes how "questions taken from interview-based attachment research tools may provide form and shape to clinical thinking" (p. 29) without unduly constraining the therapeutic relationship.

In Chapter 3, Anne Power introduces a shift of focus from the individual to the couple or, when working with an individual, to the "couple in mind". Countertransference experience is again to the fore. Early on, Power notes a patient's (Mike) "low-key and repetitive" self-presentation (p. 37) and her own corresponding zeal and over-busyness as she tries to tempt him to join her in exploration.

The main emphasis in Chapter 3 is on how these dynamics play out in a couple – and indeed on how avoidant people get together with a partner at all – and who gets together with whom when one or both of the partners has a default mode of minimisation and auto-regulation. This is the essence of the "Why would they bother?" question in the chapter title. The need and desire to become part of a couple is, as

Power describes, extremely powerful: it is what most of us look for in our lives. For avoidant individuals, however, there are countervailing forces in play. "Avoidant individuals had to adapt to caregivers who were non-reciprocal, dismissive or derogatory … As children they learned to be both self-soothing and self-stimulating, a pattern which makes adult couple relationships difficult" (p. 38).

Power explores some of the ways in which the couple relationship may play out in this paradoxical situation by way of reflection on work with individual clients Mike, Fiona, Cheryl, and a couple who came to therapy together, Sam and Gina. The latter case example offers a beautifully clear depiction of the recognisable pattern of the "worn-out pursuer" (p. 35) in relationship to the partner who consistently resists intimacy.

Power calls on research in the course of her discussion, particularly the work of Crittenden. Like Music, she references the influence of being sent to boarding school and, in addition, the need to be aware of cultural differences in childcare practice and the influence of different norms and practices on patterns of attachment.

In the final chapter of the book, Linda Cundy "outlines the core anxieties of avoidant individuals and highlights the myriad of creative strategies used to keep others at a safe emotional distance" (p. 69). These core anxieties and strategies are illustrated with case examples; three clients are presented with very different upbringings in terms of social class and relational experience, differences that are reflected in their adult trajectory and their degree of disturbance. At the most disturbed end of the spectrum is "Wes", whose attachment pattern is complex, combining elements of dismissive and disorganised attachment and considerable unresolved trauma, a presentation that will be especially familiar to readers working in forensic settings.

In discussing her work, Cundy brings to the fore the interplay between parental narcissism, shame, and avoidant attachment. Drawing on the work of Mollon (2002) she traces the way in which the authentic self can become an embarrassment and source of anxiety to the child in the face of the caring parent's lack of sensitivity to, or concern for, the child's emotional needs. In her case studies and discussion, she gives equal weight to the attachment theory emphasis on the adaptive function of the avoidant style in the external world and the object relations concern with the need to protect the internal world from fragmentation. As part of the discussion, she references the work of Bick and others on a "psychic skin" that can become toughened into a "rhinoceros hide" if that is what it takes to safeguard the internal world. There is a welcome point of contact and potential debate here between attachment and object relations points of view. Toughening, or in attachment terms dismissiveness, may or may not be adaptive in the external world – for example, it is likely to drive an intrusive mother into a state of vengeful rage. Nevertheless, it may at times be essential to psychic survival, the only possible means of defending the internal world. There is an opportunity inherent in Cundy's work for considering the experiential world of the child faced with an impossible choice of this nature and the consequences of such a "no win" situation for his or her development and wellbeing.

Drawing on contemporary attachment theory and research, Cundy proposes specific aims in therapeutic work with avoidant clients. These include a focus on feelings and affect regulation, the construction of an elaborated and coherent narrative, and the development of psychological-mindedness. From an object relations perspective, she also emphasises the importance for the client of modifying his relationship with himself, and of installing a new, secure internal object. Despite these technical recommendations, she emphasises that: "This is not a formulaic, manualised approach but a deeply relational one" (p. 96).

It was John Bowlby's firm belief that both theory and practice should be informed by sound research. Research and theory are fully present in this volume but there is nothing formulaic about the material presented here. Nowhere is there any suggestion of a "one size fits all" approach. Rather, the four authors present a picture of great complexity – complexity in the ways in which avoidance finds expression and complexity in terms of the impact on the practitioner. We may reflect also on the many changes that have occurred since the time Bowlby was writing, not least the arrival of the internet and the possibility of relating through social media. Cundy outlines how this development may interact with attachment patterns in a short section in Chapter 4.

Although only Chapter 1 presents clinical work with children, the question of parental care – or lack of care – is never far from the authors' minds. A background picture emerges of parental disappointment, rejection, intrusiveness, narcissism, or neglect. Babies do not come into the world avoidant: they learn to be avoidant. This understanding is a source of both compassion and hope: what has been learned can be unlearned. Notwithstanding the difficulties of the work, in particular the deadness in the countertransference, the commitment of the authors to these clients shines through. The lives of our avoidant clients are constricted and they fully deserve our care and commitment. As demonstrated in the clinical work that is at the heart of the text, when their defences are recognised and understood, therapeutic work can be particularly rewarding.

References

Cundy, L. (ed.) (2017). *Anxiously Attached: Understanding and Working with Preoccupied Attachment.* London: Karnac.

Farnfield, S. (2017). The Adult Attachment Interview: Information processing and the distinguishing Features of preoccupied attachment – or: What has attachment theory ever done for us? In: L. Cundy (ed.), *Anxiously Attached: Understanding and Working with Preoccupied Attachment* (pp. 43–68). London: Karnac.

Mollon, P. (2002). *Shame and Jealousy: The Hidden Turmoils.* London: Karnac.

CHAPTER ONE

Avoiding avoidance: neglecting emotional neglect and deactivated relationship styles

Graham Music

In work with children and young people we are more likely to encounter cut-off and avoidant attachment patterns than in private adult psychotherapy where very avoidant people less commonly present for help. This is the point of an avoidant attachment pattern; it gives rise to a profound belief that you have to stand on your own two feet, that seeking help is a form of weakness, that strong emotions should be avoided, particularly upsetting negative ones. For more avoidant personalities, early adaptation to their families of origin would have meant deactivating their attachment needs, because displaying their dependency and neediness would have led them to be rejected by their primary carers.

Part of my personal history was being sent to boarding school at the age of nine, where I, alongside many other boys my age, had to "just get on with life", where there was no space for moping, missing parental care, or feeling understood, or for upset or fragile emotions. Many of us developed tough defences, forms of exoskeletons that aided survival, but left the needy, often desperate, aspects of our personality deeply buried, to be avoided at all costs. The psychoanalyst Herbert Rosenfeld (1987) described a form of narcissistic defence in which the needy, dependent parts of the self are attacked and denigrated or, alternatively, projected into others and attacked there. This is in part why it is so common for an adult with a needy, ambivalently-attached way of relating to be in a relationship with someone, often a man, with a primarily avoidant style. The archetypal British "stiff upper lip" personality style is a classic example of this avoidant way of being, and of course many of the British upper classes had this reinforced by also being sent away to boarding school very early on. Indeed, some even believe that this is one of the reasons why politicians seem so deaf to young children's emotional needs (Duffell, 2000; Schaverien, 2015).

This client group can challenge conventional therapeutic technique – and challenge us personally. They evoke a range of countertransference feelings that are hard to admit to, but are the most vital clues to how we should approach the work. These include boredom, deadness, and cut off, dulled down states in which thoughts can become wooden and bodily feelings flat. I will suggest that it is easy with such patients to be unwittingly drawn into enactments (Aron, 2001) and a form of role-responsiveness (Sandler, 1993) whereby there can be two dulled people in the room and little real therapy is done.

Work with such children requires an understanding of how normal developmental trajectories might have been stymied by the lack of good experiences and how such stalled trajectories can be re-started. As Alvarez says, these children are not withdrawn but rather can be thought of as "undrawn" (Alvarez, 1992) and require a particular kind of "reclamation" or "live company" to come alive and grow a mind.

For this, a developmentally informed psychoanalytic approach (Hurry, 1998) is needed, allied with astute observational skills. Such work also requires helping patients to experience and bear positive as well as the negative emotional states that are the usual fare in psychoanalytic work (Music, 2009).

We also need to be prepared to speak with authenticity and spontaneity, as many in both the British Independent (Coltart, 1992; Klauber, 1987; Symington, 1983) and relational (Altman *et al.*, 2002; Aron, 2001; Bromberg, 1998) traditions have asserted. This avoids the dangers of over-using interpretations with such children defensively, to make one believe that one is doing something called therapy when one is in fact going through the motions.

Work with this group is also helped by facilitating interoception, the awareness of body sensations (Farb *et al.*, 2015), as too many avoidant children are cut off from the kind of body awareness that allows them to read and respond to their own signals.

A big therapeutic challenge is to remain psychologically alive and curious with children who so easily slip out of our minds. Such children and adults can be experienced as deadened, inhibited, passive, and overly self-contained. They often have little ability to reflect on emotions (their own and others'), their narrative capacity is limited, and they experience little pleasure. Indeed, they rarely inspire hope, affection, or enjoyment in those around them.

In sessions, I can find my mind wandering off. In fact, my cognitive countertransference is rarely alive with fantasies and reveries useful to the work. Rather it is my somatic countertransference that gives me the important clues – my listlessness and lack of presence, my boredom and dullness. Winnicott (1994) exhorted us to be alive to and bear our "hate in the countertransference". With these patients we might add the need to be alert to "boredom in the countertransference".

Many have not suffered terrible abuse or obvious trauma, such as being beaten, sexually abused, or witnessing violence. These children are marked out not by what happened *to* them, but rather by what *did not* happen to them – in other words, neglect. They have lacked the good experiences that foster healthy emotional development.

An example from a typical clinical day illustrates something of the response often evoked in such work. One morning my second patient is a very neglected and cut-off boy I call Josh. We do not have very much information about Josh's early life but we know he was adopted from a South American orphanage at the age of nearly three. Reports suggest that his early environment provided at best for his basic physical needs but not his emotional development. We do not know at what age he entered the orphanage or anything about his biological parents.

When the receptionist informs me of Josh's arrival I feel a deadening thud inside as I slowly reach for the phone. I walk down the corridor lethargically, nearly dragging my feet. My breathing is shallow and, indeed, so is my mind. I feel a kind of dread and am certainly not looking forward to the session. I barely remember what happened last time, but know it was very much like the session before. My main intention is to try to keep myself psychologically present. In the waiting room Josh is sitting where he sits every time, reading from the same set of comics. He looks up in the same way he always does, and I feel dulled down in the face of his predictability as he languidly gets up and follows me to the therapy room. There is a robotic feel to all this. My reactions to Josh are, I think, typical of what often happens in the presence of children who have been emotionally neglected.

This is in stark contrast to my previous patient, who I call Tommy. He is not the kind of child this chapter describes, and was overtly abused and traumatised rather than neglected. The contrast in countertransference responses between abused children like Tommy and neglected ones such as Josh is very telling. There is rarely a dull moment in therapy with Tommy. The previous week I left the session with bruised shins, a battered therapy room and my psyche similarly battered. Six-year-old Tommy cannot be still for even a few seconds. He is a real handful not only for me, but also for his teachers, his social worker, and especially his adoptive parents. Yet with Tommy, as opposed to neglected children such as Josh, I feel alive and interested. When the receptionist tells me of his arrival my heart begins to beat fast, partly from anxious sympathetic nervous system arousal, but also from a modicum of eager anticipation. Something about Tommy evokes warm feelings in those who know him, a warmth one rarely experiences in response to dulled down, more neglected children.

Troy: a case example

I describe a boy of nearly three, who I call Troy, to illustrate typical issues in working with children who have developed a very avoidant way of being, in this case linked with extreme early neglect. Troy was placed for adoption with a childless couple who had already adopted a boy a year older than Troy, who I call Alf. They had their hands full with Alf, who almost definitely had an ambivalent attachment style, was clingy, demanding, and needed constant attention. With Alf, these parents were constantly active and involved and, even if it was hard work, they had the gratification of being in no doubt how much they were needed.

With Troy things were different. They did not warm to him, and he seemed to be in his own world much of the time. He did puzzles and played with sand but did not play symbolically and, more importantly, did not seem to need people. He could ask for things such as toys or food, but seem unbothered about who he was with. He would fall over or cut himself but seek no comfort, would run off in the supermarket and not look back to his parents, and when reunited after a separation showed no pleasure, reacting to his parents just as he did to strangers. In other words, this was an extreme variant of an avoidant attachment style in which he had had to deny the emotional need of others.

Troy's history makes some sense of this. He was born into a single parent family with a depressed, learning-disabled mother who barely interacted with him. He was left in a pram on his own. He was clothed and fed and was maybe fortunate that the case was picked up by social workers as the warning signs were not obvious. He was taken into care as a one-year-old when neighbours alerted services that his mother had left him alone on several evenings. He was placed with an experienced foster carer who was looking after several children. She was efficient, the home was kept extremely clean, and again everyone was fed, clothed and changed. Troy was described as "easy to manage" and "well-adjusted". He did not protest that he was barely interacted with – Why would he? He knew nothing better and this was what he expected from life. He was left to his own devices for much of the time. Indeed, when the prospective adopters first saw him he was in a buggy with a bottle in his mouth and apparently such "prop-feeding" was normal. He had already had thousands of hours of learning not to expect very much from adults.

In my first meeting, the parents conveyed many worries. Alf always required one parent's attention in the session, while Troy wandered around the room. It was probably twenty-five minutes before I realised that I, a child psychotherapist trained to be in touch with children's minds and feelings, was barely paying him any attention, and nor was anyone else. He had slipped out of our minds. Even when there was awareness of his physical needs, any idea of him as a human being with thoughts or an emotional world seemed to get lost.

I decided to begin to engage in dyadic work (Hughes, 2007) with Troy and whichever parent could bring him. I also did some modelling for them by staying close to him and watching what he did and talking aloud about this. Any hint of a more interactive gesture that I saw, such as Troy reaching out or looking quizzical, I hammed up and amplified. I broke my usual pattern and became more directive, suggesting that each parent took time alone at home with Troy every day, since it was apparent that when they were all together Alf commandeered their attention and Troy, who seemed to need little, was indeed given little.

The model I had in my mind, which I often refer to in similar cases, comes from Selma Fraiberg's (1974) work with blind babies and sighted mothers. Fraiberg helped these mothers draw their infants into an interpersonal world by pointing out the infants' barely noticeable reactions: their faces might not have lit up in response to their mothers' voices but a little toe wiggle here and hand gesture there were taken as signs that the mothers were important to their infants. This encouraged the mothers to interact more vigorously and the babies in turn responded, becoming livelier and, importantly, more fulfilling to look after.

This is just what happened with Troy's parents, who within a few weeks were coming into sessions with stories of little changes he was making. I was moved and indeed close to tears one session when I played with him, observing and talking about what he was doing; I caught a fleeting gesture in which he momentarily pointed at an object and looked at me. This was an example of what we call "proto-declarative pointing", in which a child points something out knowing that this thing, in this case a picture, would be in the other person's mind too, that two people can share an appreciation of this third object, and know they are sharing it. This let me know that he was not on course to be on the autistic spectrum; we had in that moment shared what autistic children never do, a genuinely intersubjective moment when we both knew what was in the other's mind and could enjoy and appreciate this.

His mother watched me interact with him and slowly got interested in him, and he responded to this. In a session a few weeks later he was tapping the table and she said: "Oh look at that tapping, you are anxious aren't you". This felt miraculous. She had noted and ascribed emotional meaning to an action that a few weeks before would have gone unnoticed. This is how infants develop a sense both of being held in mind and getting to know their own thoughts and feelings. Slowly this flat and cut-off boy became more lively, interested, and fun-loving.

After a few months, Troy began to play peekaboo, and would shriek with delight when found, wanting more and more attention. After a while, another moment signified a change. He stumbled in the room and tripped up and hit his head, but this time instead of just getting up as if nothing had happened he looked up at his mother and his hands for a second seemed to reach out to her. This was the beginning of normal secure attachment behaviour, an expression of his need for her. Mother was deeply touched by this.

Another sign of this was when I introduced Troy, in the presence of his mother, to a gifted clinical psychologist who was to do play therapy alongside our family work. In the room, he cuddled into his mother for safety, showing the first signs we had seen of appropriate attachment behaviour in the face of stranger anxiety. Only a few months before he would have carried on as if nothing significant had happened. In fact, he responded very well to the play therapy as well as to the family work and it was important that the parents could see the effects of what they were doing.

Within a few more months Troy was remarkably transformed, so much so that his parents even worried that he was getting rather rowdy! He had begun to scream to demand attention, was being a rival with his brother, made a huge noise if he felt he was being ignored and was most definitely a lively little boy who knew he had needs and was extremely ready to express them.

At the point of referral, the parents were in a crisis and had decided that they probably were not going to keep Troy. Indeed, his would-be mother admitted at a review at the end of the treatment that in those early days she had thought every day about giving him up. Maybe one child was enough, they had reasoned, and anyway it was probably not fair on Alf who needed lots of attention. The truth was probably that they did not feel sufficient warmth for Troy, nor could they enjoy parenting him. By the end they felt warmth, and he felt warmth; indeed, I did too.

Troy was typical of many avoided and neglected children in not evoking warmth or affection in those around him. We need to feel we are needed if we are to parent well or offer other forms of help to a child, and these children often act as if they don't need us or anyone, making us feel useless. By the end of the therapy, not only Troy, but also his parents and Alf all seemed very different. I think the parents felt affection, love, and passion for Troy, and would have fought to keep him. The work with Troy was easier than in many cases as he was so young and retained much developmental potential. Nonetheless his story was all too typical and could easily have ended disastrously, with a string of foster placements and Troy growing into a cold, cut-off young person.

Psychoanalytic thinking

In thinking about avoidance we can build on helpful psychoanalytic ideas about "cut off" and un-psychologically minded patients. In adult psychoanalysis, Bollas (1987) uses the concept "normotic" to describe patients he sees as psychologically "unborn", who he found were often raised in families where their "real selves" were not mirrored, with parents not alive to their children's inner reality. Bollas describes normotic patients as having little capacity for identification or empathy and as "strangely objectless". With them, our words spoken with meaning, life, and energy can quickly become denuded of significance. These are not patients who are attacking links in Bion's (1959) sense, but rather links have simply not developed, something which seems to be corroborated by recent neuroscience (Siegel, 2012).

McDougall (1992) describes similar patients she calls "normopaths", often alexythmic patients who lack an affective or interior life or "personal psychic theatres" (p. 156). Her writing about such patients is full of metaphors such as "armour plated shells". She argues that it can take years before such "rejected representations and stifled affects which surround this sterilised space become available to verbal thought and psychic elaboration" (p. 443).

In clinical writings about such patients there is often an almost despairing thread about how the therapist is affected. Ogden (1999) writes that one's sense of aliveness or deadness is the central measure of the status of the therapy. He argues that the analyst has to work hard to be honest about the countertransference in order to generate ways of relating meaningfully. He writes with candour about, for example, fantasies of feigning illness "to escape the stagnant deadness of the sessions" (Ogden, 1999, p. 31). I certainly find that such patients give rise to similar "heart-sink" moments. Flat inner worlds, lack of fantasy and imaginary play, and little empathy can make for unrewarding sessions.

In child psychotherapy, much writing about autistic spectrum patients is directly relevant. Several psychoanalytic writers have focussed on the need for a more "active" technique, the use of an enlivening "reclamation" (Alvarez, 1992), as well as the importance of not colluding with lifeless and empty behaviour (Alvarez and Reid, 1999; Rhode and Klauber, 2004).

Neglected children have received little attention from their parents and caregivers. They then suffer from what the child psychotherapist Gianna Henry calls "double-deprivation" (Henry, 2004), as they tragically do not use or even recognise the existence of helpfulness in the adults in their lives. In fact, we often also see what Louise Emanuel (2002) calls "triple deprivation", as these children can also get ignored or neglected by other adults and professionals. These are the children sitting in the back of class causing no trouble but almost vegetating, while all the attention goes to the bright sharp ones, or the acting out misbehaving ones.

A view from developmental science

From the works of Lou Sander (Sander *et al.*, 1972, Sander 2008), Daniel Stern (1985), and onwards, infancy research has, in recent decades, outlined the conditions for optimal emotional development. Even though there remain debates about exactly what children need – and although there are huge cultural differences about exactly what constitutes good parenting (Keller, 2007; Music, 2016) – we know much more about the effects of particular early experiences. We know which kinds of parenting lead to secure attachment, and that various forms of emotional trauma give rise to specific psychobiological effects. We know that infant minds grow in response to attuned and emotionally sensitive caregiving, that mind-minded (Meins et al., 2002) input from parents and emotional responsiveness give rise to a host of hopeful developments. This includes secure attachment and the capacity for self-regulation (Bakermans-Kranenburg et al., 2008; Fonagy et al., 2004; Schore, 2005). We know that babies need to have their difficult feelings understood, and that they feel held and contained when they know they are in the presence of adults who are trying to understand them.

This is, of course, partly why the work of psychoanalytically informed infancy researchers such as Beebe (Beebe and Lachmann, 2002), Tronick (2007), and Stern (1985) has been so important. Experimental situations have proven what we have long known from the traditions of infant observation (Bick, 1968; Miller, 1989): that being held in mind is a growth-enhancing experience. Children, of course, thrive not through having perfect care, but through experiencing a relationship in which the other person is sensitive to them and tries to repair mismatches and get miscommunications back on track.

Such repairs give rise to a sense of agency in infants and children (Alvarez, 1992; Broucek, 1991). They learn that if something goes wrong it is not the end of the world. They come to believe that repair is possible, that they can play a part in facilitating this and are players in relationships. This links with the emphasis relational psychoanalysts place on becoming aware of enactments and stepping outside of them. With avoidant and/or neglected children who have lacked attuned early experiences, the therapist's feelings of dullness or boredom, and consequent lack of active responsiveness to the patient, can be viewed as a form of enactment.

Throughout the first year of life, in cases where care is good enough, imitative capacities transform into more sophisticated mutual understanding. By just four months infants come to know they are the object of another's attention, showing coyness, for example (Reddy, 2000), and, with luck, by eight months they can attain sufficient understanding of other minds to be able to "tease and muck about" (Reddy, 2008). By about nine months "joint attention" and what Trevarthen (Trevarthen and Hubley, 1978) originally called secondary intersubjectivity are in place, as well as the building blocks of empathy (Decety et al., 2012), altruism (Tomasello, 2009), and mutuality. This is all built on early reciprocity and what Anne Alvarez, after Colwyn Trevarthen, called "live company" (Alvarez, 1992), something so many neglected children lack.

Such experiences, incrementally built up over the seconds, minutes, hours, and then days, weeks, months, and years of a young life, are what give rise to an internal world full of richness and trust and interest in the external world. Infants are born other-centred (Bråten, 2006) as opposed to ego-centred. Or, as Emde might put it, an ego depends on first forming a "we-go" (Emde, 2009). We might be born with a preconception of what Trevarthen (2001) calls a "companion in meaning making", but if reality does not deliver such companionship then infants adapt to their reality, however bleak. They quickly learn that there is not much to be expected or hoped for from human relationships and can retreat to cut-off emotional styles that we associate with avoidance.

Lucy

Lucy demonstrated many of the classic "deactivated" attachment characteristics. Lucy was 14 years old and had been coming to see me for about nine months. She initially had anorexic symptoms, although these had abated. She was a challenge to work with, especially because she was cut off from emotions and in fact I often felt a bit spaced out with her. For a long time, she was unremittingly positive, in a way that felt less than real, and indeed rather dull. We see this a lot in people with avoidant attachment, which is another way of thinking about children like Lucy.

She was thin and also pale, quiet and distant. Her manner was often diminishing of what I said, even if she did this in the nicest possible way. For example, when I would try to think about something that might have been bothering her, maybe a friendship issue, she would say things like, "Oh, that's normal", or "Of course". I felt that I was being a bit silly trying to say anything emotionally alive to her. This often left me feeling that I was being like her mother forcing food down her when she was not hungry, which was in fact what used to happen at home. I think she came to see me compliantly, because other people were saying she should, and there was a wary passivity about her. Not surprisingly I did not especially look forward to our sessions.

Before one session, about which I now describe fragments, she smiled as she saw me in the waiting room, but as usual it was hard to know how placatory the smile was. She came in and looked awkwardly away and did not say anything. After a silence, I said that it is difficult to speak and she nodded. She started, in her slightly distant way, recounting a few events of the week, which seemed in fact quite uneventful. When I tried to open things up I felt parried, as usual very nicely, as she insisted that everything was fine and that she was happy and that, in fact, she was determined to be happy.

I asked again how she had been. She looked at me and said *"Fine"*, and I looked back at her, hamming up a quizzical and disbelieving expression; she was already laughing. We had a narrative by now; she knew I would call her on her "fineness", that I did not really believe in it. I simply said *"Fine"*, a bit sarcastically, and she said *"Yeah fine"*. I then said *"Fine in what way I wonder"*, tongue in cheek, and she said *"Fine, just fine"*, a bit teasing of me, slightly self-mockingly. She laughed, and I joined in, we had made contact but were far away from real emotional relating.

Feelings had never been talked about at home and she had learnt to cut off from them. I talked about how hard it is to come here and said: *"How do you feel when you are sitting here, like now, and do not know what to say. Do you feel nervous, worried, or maybe cross or embarrassed, I wonder?"*. She replied *"Weird"*, and I asked in what way and she said *"Just weird"*; I replied *"Uh huh"*. I said: *"So this is what happens, I ask a question or say something, I try to inject feeling into this* (I intone a strength of feelings, like an engine revving*), and then I get a one-word response, and I feel I go like this* (making a noise like air coming out of a balloon)." She smiles. I feel something has got through, she actually giggles and slightly relaxes. I thought some colour came to her cheeks. However, I also worried that she felt told off, that she hears me as suggesting that she is not good enough. I said: *"I am not surprised really, you have had a lifetime of practising being bright and breezy with no difficult feelings, there is little room for those in the family I know, they are an alien and awkward interference."*

As is already clear, Lucy is quite emotionally detached, cut off or dampened down. I had to work quite hard to inject life into the sessions. I used sarcasm a bit; sometimes it helped but it can also backfire. I said that I did not believe that she had nothing to say about what had happened in the week, whether good or bad. She mumbled something about her friend coming to her drama class. I asked about this and she looked at me as if she had said enough, rather like I imagine she might feel if she has eaten enough. I said, with as much feeling as I could muster, *"You really can't believe that I'm interested in you can you, in how you feel, or that I might care about how and what you feel?"* A flicker of emotion ran across her face, as if she was startled, even touched. I said, *"Feelings are a bit of a foreign country, especially the idea that yours might be important and of interest, to me, and others close to you."* She looked at me and then away, as if that was a bit intense but nevertheless I felt that she was glad of what I had said.

She then told me about her friend who is joining her class at school, saying they have a lot in common. I asked about this and she had to dig deep to try to find any words to describe how she feels and what she thinks. Once again, I had to be careful not to be too forceful. She told me that they have the same taste in things like clothes and music and boys. I said, *"And boys"* and she retorted *"Justin Bieber"*; I then said *"Not real ones then?"* and she replied *"He is real"* – clearly, I had been drawn into something a bit too chatty and jokey. I also know that what for most young people is no more than casual conversation is, for Lucy, the start of genuine autobiographical narrative and self-reflection. It might not feel like much but this was progress.

I took a risk and asked if her friend had been worried about her. This was an attempt to develop mentalising, to see things from another's perspective. She told me a story about some physical exercise she had been doing. Other girls said that she was doing this to lose weight but this friend had said that she was "well fit". I asked what it was like to have people worry about her and said that maybe it can feel like pressure. She said that it is different when it is a friend than when it is parents. She told me that she wanted to change things and she wished that she was not like she was, that when others asked for ice cream she would ask not to have any. It was stupid, she said, and she just wanted to get taller, and stop all this and to change. I found myself touched, emotionally present, which was unusual. I said that it did not sound to me as if things were at all fine, but that in fact she had been very unhappy. I had to force myself to say these things because of the jokey atmosphere and her constant smiling.

I tried to stay with the difficult feelings and I asked more about them. She told me about having bad thoughts at night, and that she has felt like giving up. I felt genuine concern and explored further. She was able to admit that she had had thoughts about self-harm and wishing she were not alive. I, of course, explored whether these were thoughts I should be worried about. The danger of exploring the potential risk with her was that she might feel I could not bear the depth of her feelings, so I had to be very clear about how she needed me to know just how awful she had felt.

She then needed a bit of a breather and a few minutes later said again that she wanted to stop being how she was and be normal. I talked about how she seemed to really want that at times but that there is another part of her, an anorexic part, which also has a lot of power and does not want things to change. I wonder what that part of her might have to say today. She found it hard to say anything about this and I decided to make guesses, saying, for example, *"Maybe it says don't trust that idiot and anyway, rely on yourself; his thoughts, like food, are just not good for you."* She laughed at this and again there was a slight flush to her face as if she felt caught out and was not sure how much she liked it. She did say that the anorexic voice was the "strongest" one then immediately tried to backtrack, as if she had revealed an important secret. Soon we were back to her sitting, fiddling around, playing with her watch, legs moving up and down, and me trying to prompt her. I tried to gently tease her about this, but to no avail. I felt that I had got too near to real issues, but here at least was actual emotional material to build on.

She did then let me know that at night she worried that everything is going to go wrong. I was getting a sense of the depth of her anxiety; she was riddled with it, and it is not surprising she had to cut off from it. She said that she had to get out of bed in the night and that a voice told her what to do. She said: *"It must sound mad"*. I asked about other habits and she told me that she has to have everything completely tidy in her room, and that when her mother was making her bed she watched carefully to make sure that no bits were sticking out because they cannot be. Here were her first revelations of obsessional traits that would feature in the ensuing weeks.

I talked about how the way she always says "fine" is a bit like tidying everything up, and that maybe it is scary to talk about things that might seem a bit messy emotionally. She told me about a friend who is very like her and for this friend everything has an exact place and that they have been brought up similarly and understand everything about each other and what they think. I tried to explore this, both the backgrounds and how they were similar but this rather petered out. It was getting towards the end of the session. She was fiddling around, playing with her feet and her watch, which was swinging. I glanced at it as was swinging and said, "*Hypnotising me?*"; in a flash she was smiling and swinging it more. I was struck by how easy it was to get into a jokey almost flirtatious rapport. I noted again that there was something almost cruel in the quick-wittedness and it certainly successfully pushed away feelings.

There was more silence and I noted how hard she found it to speak but, despite that, she had spoken more than she thought she would, and that it does take some courage when she is not used to it.

Some months later Lucy said she was ready to stop. She told me very forcefully that she was not anorexic anymore, that she has not got a problem. She said her parents are getting tired of her coming and that she does not want to come and does not want to be viewed as someone who has a problem. She wants to be just like a normal adolescent. She wanted to tell me about a more coping assertive Lucy who was managing a lot of things very well. In some ways, this seemed to be the case, as she had managed to find a central place in a popular group of friends, to be doing very well at her singing and dancing. She clearly wanted to take her place as a "normal adolescent", which seems to mean one who does not have problems, does not want to talk about feelings, and really wants to just fit in. Nonetheless, I of course felt worried that this was something of what Freud called a "flight into health".

Still, maybe the most hopeful thing was her tone of voice, how she could be so clear. There was no false looking after me. She said she thought that the reason that she had got better was because of her friends, and it was not her mum, or (I need to add) coming here. Another courageous thing to say. I thought that she was going off to be determinedly happy and that there was not really any space for reflecting on emotional experience, but also felt that she had had a good experience and would return to therapy, if she needed it, later in adolescence.

In Lucy's final session, I asked about what had happened over the last year that had been important and she did say that the main difference was that, "*I am not unhappy anymore, and I eat now*". It was also possible to talk about how she felt that she had grown up, was now getting on better at home, and indeed the whole family were getting on better, and that she was able to manage her relationships at school much better as well. I did not get any sense that she felt that any of this was anything to do with the therapy.

She went on to tell me about some of the things happening in her life, such as dancing in some big shows and a possible television appearance. Her most lively and in touch moments were when she was talking about friends and, in particular, the boy she was now *"going out with"*. She was able to show me that she was in fact not finding it easy that he had *"blanked"* her this morning, and that he had not returned her last text message. It felt that any transference implications needed to remain in my mind, although I did try to talk about how she might worry that she not will remain in my mind. This was greeted with a certain amount of derision, but she looked away, and down at her phone, and I felt that she was touched and knew she had been touched by our work. She told me with a certain amount of bravado that boys are *"not worth worrying about"*, but in fact she could let me know that she had dared to really open herself up this time. She said touchingly: *"I am a worrier, like my mum, she worries about everything."* She talked about the difference from when she was in year 7, when with boys it was *"dump them in a week"*. I thought of how dumped I had felt in the early sessions by her powerfully denigratory avoidant attachment style, and how this contrasted with a young woman who, at least some of the time, was now in touch with thoughts and feelings, and who I not only cared about, but who I knew cared about the fact that I cared about her. Of course, I remained concerned about various aspects, such as her tendency to retreat under stress to denying having any worries in her life, her pseudo-independence, obsessional features, and propensity for not straight-forward eating. Nonetheless, she had had the new experience of being with someone else who could think about all of her and tolerate her emotional states, and there was now at least the capacity for emotionally alive and engaged interaction.

Attachment avoidance and emotional deactivation

Lucy is a classic case of how any of us can develop a somewhat stunted ability to become aware of emotions when the important people around us show us that they are not interested in our emotional needs. When our attachment figures cannot tolerate us being demonstrative, needy, or unhappy, as children we tend to shut off from these needs and wishes. As with Lucy we often then learn to become very independent and to stand on our own two feet. By shutting off from our own needs we can remain close enough to our parents or caregivers without alienating them. The cost is that we disavow aspects of ourselves and, in effect, shut down some of the richest aspects of human life.

Mary Ainsworth (Ainsworth *et al.*, 1978) devised the Strange Situation test to observe how a toddler responds to being separated from its mother and reunited with her in an unfamiliar laboratory setting. When the mother leaves the room it might look like children with an avoidant style do not mind the fact that she has gone, but in fact their heart rate goes up in a very similar way to a secure child who cries out in distress. What this suggests is that somewhere inside them they are feeling upset, at least at a bodily level, but it is as if such bodily signals have not got through, they have had to be cut off from them. Of course, this cutting off is well out of consciousness, but it was signs of this that I was trying to pick up in Lucy.

Lucy showed that classic avoidant attachment pattern of presenting as emotionally un-nuanced, superficially sensible, often refusing to be anything other than positive, and difficult to make emotional contact with or work with therapeutically. Those with more dismissing, avoidant styles seem to show brain activity suggesting a tendency to withdraw from rather than approach others, and also to be less aroused by emotional stimuli (Kungl *et al.*, 2016). This in turn influences those in their proximity. Interestingly, just listening to more dismissive attachment-related discourses leaves listeners less interested in other people's emotions and with a heightened activity of brain networks involved in social aversion (Krause *et al.*, 2016). A long-term study looking at 22-year-olds who as infants had withdrawn, depressed mothers (Moutsiana *et al.*, 2015) found them more prone to emotional control via top-down brain regions and less able to genuinely experience positive emotion. Such dismissing attachment styles give rise to a superficially positive narrative with statements such as, "Yes, my parents were really good". Children with avoidant dismissing styles tend to paint a picture of themselves as strong and self-sufficient and have a falsely positive view of their attachment figures, but one not backed up by their actual emotional experience (Borelli *et al.*, 2013). These children under-report difficult emotions, and are less aware of having any themselves, but research shows there is a profound divergence between what they say they are feeling (e.g. "everything is fine") and how they actually behave (Borelli *et al.*, 2017).

This dampening down of affects comes powerfully into our work with such children and adults, making them extremely difficult to work with. One way of understanding those children who show very avoidant and cut-off presentations, and the adults they become, is that they have a dominance of certain brain regions and networks normally associated with the left hemisphere. Their capacity for logic is much more enhanced than for emotions. Interestingly, Lucy's best subject at school was maths, which is not uncommon. Another way of thinking about these children and adults is that they have what are called "schizoid" defences, retreating into a cut-off shelter or retreat away from the real world of live powerful emotions and needs.

Iain McGilchrist (2010) has helped us understand this in terms of the functioning of the brain. While there is no simple left–right hemisphere split between rationality and emotionality, our two hemispheres generally do interpret and interact with the world in different ways. New experiences are processed more in the right hemisphere; it is the right hippocampus that is working away in response to novelty and in the right hemisphere that hormones are released such as noradrenaline, which help manage new experiences. The kinds of emotional skills central to therapy, such as empathy, primarily occur through the right hemisphere; we see another person as a feelingful whole person and identify with their experiences. After strokes in the right-sided temporoparietal area, McGilchrist shows that patients tend to have a lack of purpose and interest and indeed feeling for their body, as the right parietal lobe is central to body sense, while the left hemisphere tends to treat the body more as a mechanical thing.

Interestingly, we just cannot trust the left hemisphere all that much; it controls verbal discourse and has on its side language, logic, and linearity. According to McGilchrist, it is the "Berlusconi of the brain, a political heavyweight who has control of the media" (2010, p. 229) and whose propaganda is very convincing. The neuroscientist Michael Gazzaniga, who has done much research with split-brained patients, has called it the "left hemisphere interpreter" or storyteller. It has less interest in truth than logic, is also an inveterate denier of any reality it does not want to acknowledge, and fosters optimism in a rather ludicrous, we might say omniscient, way. McGilchrist and others argue that the right hemisphere acts as a kind of "bull-shit detector" via its use of bodily sense, intuition, and emotions. Antonio Damasio (1999) pointed to something similar when he described the importance of what he calls "somatic markers", that *felt* sense that something is not right, the knowledge that the right hemisphere has which has little to do with logic. It is no coincidence that people such as Lucy are so out of touch with their emotions and bodies given how, as Antonio Damasio has taught us, emotions are bodily processes.

As Allan Schore has helped us see over many years, the right brain develops earlier than the left in infancy, is central for empathy, emotional regulation and creativity, and is much more tuned in to body states. With left hemisphere dominance one sees much higher levels of optimism, often unwarranted, as in avoidant attachment.

Conclusions

Many avoidant children I have worked with have not undergone complete personality transformations through therapy, although the younger they are when they are offered help the more dramatic are the changes seen, as in Troy's case. They often slowly "warm up", get livelier and slightly more real. Parallel work with parents is crucial in learning to identify and amplify any slight developmental signs, which in turn can lead to more rewarding experiences. Sometimes parents, teachers, and therapists might not be pleased that our work leads to children moving from being dull and cut off to becoming more lively, aggressive, and challenging, but at least some life is forming. Such children do not generally inspire passion and therapeutic zeal, and have not only been neglected emotionally in their early lives, but are often further neglected later by other adults and professionals. If we do not provide them with the help they need, their prognosis is particularly bad. Such children so badly need from us what they also rarely evoke – our passion, interest, enjoyment, and zeal. They can leave carers and professionals feeling de-skilled, dehumanised, even bored or apathetic. Often, they do not have much awareness of minds and mental states, of stories and imagination, struggle with emotional expression, have little sense of agency, and maybe most importantly, lack much capacity for ordinary enjoyment.

Field *et al.* (2006) compared the infants of withdrawn depressed mothers with infants who suffered intrusive parenting. Those with withdrawn depressed mothers were less exploratory at the age of one, and by age of three were not showing empathy, were passive and withdrawn, and were doing worse cognitively. Intrusion is at least stimulating whereas neglect is deadening. We are born with "preconceptions" as Bion (1962) stated or, in another language, we start life experience "expectant" and if such an "evolutionarily-expectable environment" (Cicchetti and Valentino, 2006) is absent then certain capacities simply do not develop.

This group of children pose a puzzle for therapeutic work. I have suggested that with them we need to find a way to encourage agency and positive affect, and have the paradoxical task of stepping back from a lifeless encounter in order empathically to be in touch with them. With them we walk a delicate tightrope between being there to amplify aliveness, while not being intrusive. Similarly, we need to find a way to foster a sense of agency and enjoyment, while being neither too manic nor seductive. Our countertransference is always central to such work, particularly bearing uncomfortable experiences and not being taken over by a numbing atmosphere. A big challenge is ensuring that our interventions are infused with emotional aliveness, relying less than usual on more cognitively based levels of work (Alvarez, 2012).

Such "undrawn" children deserve to have adults in their lives who can find passion and bring them alive and into the world of interpersonal riches.

References

Ainsworth, M.D.S., Blehar, M.C., Waters, E., and Wall, S. (1978), *Patterns of Attachment: A Psychological Study of the Strange Situation*. Hillsdale, NJ: Erlbaum.
Altman, N., Briggs, R., Frankel, J., and Gensler, D. (2002). *Relational Child Psychotherapy*. New York: Other Press.
Alvarez, A. (1992). *Live Company*. Hove, UK: Routledge.
Alvarez, A. (2012). *The Thinking Heart: Three Levels of Psychoanalytic Therapy with Disturbed Children*. Hove, UK: Routledge.
Alvarez, A. and Reid, S. (1999). *Autism and Personality: Findings from the Tavistock Autism Workshop*. 1st edn. Hove, UK: Routledge.
Aron, L. (2001). *A Meeting of Minds: Mutuality in Psychoanalysis*. New York: Analytic Press.
Bakermans-Kranenburg, M.J., van IJzendoorn, M., Mesman, J., Alink, L.R.A., and Juffer, F. (2008). Effects of an attachment-based intervention on daily cortisol moderated by dopamine receptor D4: A randomized control trial on 1- to 3-year-olds screened for externalizing behavior. *Development and Psychopathology*, 20(3), pp. 805–820.
Beebe, B. and Lachmann, F.M. (2002). *Infant Research and Adult Treatment: Co-Constructing Interactions*. New York: Analytic Press.
Bick, E. (1968). The experience of the skin in early object relations. *International Journal of Psycho-Analysis*, 49, pp. 484–486.
Bion, W.R. (1959). Attacks on linking. *International Journal of Psycho-Analysis*, 40(5–6), p. 308.
Bion, W.R. (1962). *Learning from Experience*. London: Heinemann.
Bollas, C. (1987). *The Shadow of the Object: Psychoanalysis of the Unthought Known*. London: Free Association.

Borelli, J.L., David, D.H., Crowley, M.J., Snavely, J.E., and Mayes, L.C. (2013). Dismissing children's perceptions of their emotional experience and parental care: Preliminary evidence of positive bias. *Child Psychiatry & Human Development*, 44(1), pp. 70–88.

Borelli, J.L., Ho, L.C., Sohn, L., Epps, L., Coyiuto, M., and West, J.L. (2017). School-aged children's attachment dismissal prospectively predicts divergence of their behavioral and self-reported anxiety. *Journal of Child and Family Studies*, 26(4), pp. 1018–1028.

Bråten, S. (ed.) (2006). *Intersubjective Communication and Emotion in Early Ontogeny*. New edn. Cambridge: Cambridge University Press.

Bromberg, P.M. (1998). *Standing in the Spaces: Essays on Clinical Process, Trauma, and Dissociation*. New York: Analytic Press.

Broucek, F.J. (1991). *Shame and the Self*. New York: The Guilford Press.

Cicchetti, D. and Valentino, K. (2006). An ecological-transactional perspective on child maltreatment: Failure of the average expectable environment and its influence on child development. In: D. Cicchetti and D. Cohen (eds.), *Developmental Psychopathology: Risk, Disorder, and Adaptation* (pp. 129–201). New York: Wiley.

Coltart, N. (1992). *Slouching Towards Bethlehem*. London: Free Association Books.

Damasio, A.R. (1999). *The Feeling of What Happens: Body, Emotion and the Making of Consciousness*. London: Heineman.

Decety, J., Norman, G.J., Berntson, G.G., and Cacioppo, J.T. (2012). A neurobehavioral evolutionary perspective on the mechanisms underlying empathy. *Progress in Neurobiology*, 98(1), pp. 38–48.

Duffell, N. (2000). *The Making of Them: The British Attitude to Children and the Boarding School System*. London: Lone Arrow Press.

Emanuel, L. (2002). Deprivation × 3. *Journal of Child Psychotherapy*, 28(2), pp. 163–179.

Emde, R.N. (2009). From ego to "we-go": Neurobiology and questions for psychoanalysis: Commentary on papers by Trevarthen, Gallese, and Ammaniti & Trentini. *Psychoanalytic Dialogues*, 19(5), pp. 556–564.

Farb, N., Daubenmier, J., Price, C.J., Gard, T., Kerr, C., Dunn, B.D., Klein, A.C., Paulus, M.P., and Mehling, W.E. (2015). Interoception, contemplative practice, and health. *Frontiers in Psychology*, 6, p. 763.

Field, T., Diego, M., and Hernandez-Reif, M. (2006). Prenatal depression effects on the fetus and newborn: A review. *Infant Behavior and Development*, 29(3), pp. 445–455.

Fonagy, P., Gyorgy, G., Jurist, E.L., and Target, M. (2004). *Affect Regulation, Mentalization, and the Development of the Self*. London: Karnac.

Fraiberg, S. (1974). Blind infants and their mothers: An examination of the sign system. In: M. Lewis and L.A. Rosenblum (eds.), *The Effect of the Infant on its Caregiver* (pp. 215–232). Oxford: Wiley.

Gazzaniga, M.S., 2005. Forty-five years of split-brain research and still going strong. *Nature Reviews Neuroscience*, 6, 653–659.
Henry, G. (2004). Doubly deprived. In: P. Barrows (ed.), *Key Papers from the Journal of Child Psychotherapy* (pp. 105–120). Hove, UK: Brunner-Routledge.
Hughes, D.A. (2007). *Attachment-Focused Family Therapy*. 1st edn. New York: Norton.
Hurry, A. (1998). *Psychoanalysis and Developmental Therapy*. London: Karnac.
Keller, H. (2007). *Cultures of Infancy*. Mahwah, NJ: Lawrence Erlbaum.
Klauber, J. (1987). *Illusion and Spontaneity in Psychoanalysis*. London: Free Association.
Krause, A.L., Borchardt, V., Li, M., van Tol, M-J., Demenescu, L.R., Strauss, B., Kirchmann, H., Buchheim, A., Metzger, C.D., Nolte, T., and Walter, M. (2016). Dismissing attachment characteristics dynamically modulate brain networks subserving social aversion. *Frontiers in Human Neuroscience* (online), 10. Available at: www.ncbi.nlm.nih.gov/pmc/articles/PMC4783398/ (accessed 5 January 2017).
Kungl, M.T., Leyh, R., and Spangler, G. (2016). Attachment representations and brain asymmetry during the processing of autobiographical emotional memories in late adolescence. *Frontiers in Human Neuroscience* (online), 10. Available at: http://journal.frontiersin.org/article/10.3389/fnhum.2016.00644/abstract (accessed 5 January 2017).
McDougall, J. (1992). *Plea for A Measure of Abnormality*. 1st edn. London: Taylor & Francis.
McGilchrist, I. (2010). *The Master and His Emissary: The Divided Brain and the Making of the Western World*. New Haven, CT: Yale University Press.
Meins, E., Fernyhough, C., Wainwright, R., Gupta, M.D., Fradley, E., and Tuckey, M. (2002). Maternal mind-mindedness and attachment security as predictors of theory of mind understanding. *Child Development*, 73(6), pp. 1715–1726.
Miller, L. (1989). *Closely Observed Infants*. London: Duckworth.
Moutsiana, C., Johnstone, T., Murray, L., Fearon, P., Cooper, P.J., Pliatsikas, C., Goodyer, I., and Halligan, S.L. (2015). Insecure attachment during infancy predicts greater amygdala volumes in early adulthood. *Journal of Child Psychology and Psychiatry*, 56(5), pp. 540–548.
Music, G. (2009). What has psychoanalysis got to do with happiness? Reclaiming the positive in psychoanalytic psychotherapy. *British Journal of Psychotherapy*, 25(4), pp. 435–455.
Music, G. (2016). *Nurturing Natures: Attachment and Children's Emotional, Social and Brain Development*. London: Psychology Press.
Ogden, T.H. (1999). *Reverie and Interpretation: Sensing Something Human*. London: Karnac.
Reddy, V. (2000). Coyness in early infancy. *Developmental Science*, 3(2), pp. 186–192.

Reddy, V. (2008). *How Infants Know Minds*. Cambridge, MA: Harvard University Press.

Rhode, M. and Klauber, T. (2004). *The Many Faces of Asperger's Syndrome*. London: Karnac.

Rosenfeld, H.A. (1987). *Impasse and Interpretation: Therapeutic and Antitherapeutic Factors in the Psychoanalytic Treatment of Psychotic, Borderline, and Neurotic Patients*. London: Routledge.

Sander, L. (2008). *Living Systems, Evolving Consciousness, and the Emerging Person: A Selection of Papers from the Life Work of Louis Sander*. Hove, UK: The Analytic Press.

Sander, L., Julia, H., Steichler, G., and Burns, P. (1972). Continuous 24-hour interactional monitoring in infants reared in two caretaking environments. *Psychosomatic Medicine*, 34(3), pp. 270–282.

Sandler, J. (1993). On communication from patient to analyst: Not everything is projective identification. *International Journal of Psycho-Analysis*, 74, pp. 1097–1107.

Schaverien, J. (2015). *Boarding School Syndrome: The Psychological Trauma of the "Privileged" Child*. Hove, UK: Routledge.

Schore, A.N. (2005). Back to basics attachment, affect regulation, and the developing right brain: Linking developmental neuroscience to pediatrics. *Pediatrics in Review*, 26(6), pp. 204–217.

Siegel, D.J. (2012). *The Developing Mind: Toward a Neurobiology of Interpersonal Experience*. New York: The Guilford Press.

Stern, D.N. (1985). *The Interpersonal World of the Infant*. New York: Basic Books.

Symington, N. (1983). The analyst's act of freedom as agent of therapeutic change. *International Review of Psycho-Analysis*, 10, pp. 283–291.

Tomasello, M. (2009). *Why We Cooperate*. Cambridge, MA: MIT Press.

Trevarthen, C. (2001). Intrinsic motives for companionship in understanding: Their origin, development, and significance for infant mental health. *Infant Mental Health Journal*, 22(1–2), pp. 95–131.

Trevarthen, C. and Hubley, P. (1978). Secondary intersubjectivity: Confidence, confiding and acts of meaning in the first year. In: A. Lock (ed.), *Action, Gesture and Symbol: The Emergence of Language* (pp. 183–229). London: Academic Press.

Tronick, E. (2007). *The Neurobehavioral and Social Emotional Development of Infants and Children*. New York: Norton.

Winnicott, D.W. (1994). Hate in the counter-transference. *Journal of Psychotherapy Practice and Research*, 3(4), p. 348.

CHAPTER TWO

Not trying to avoid the bridge: avoidant attachment from research to clinical practice

Andrea Oskis

Attachment theory offers a powerful framework for understanding relationships across the lifespan. It clearly connects early parenting experiences with subsequent risks of clinical difficulties. This model of what it is to be human, and the contributions of John Bowlby and Mary Ainsworth, have been invaluable to both clinical and research fields regarding attachment. Yet "translating" research and evidence into clinical practice is an ongoing, sometimes problematic, and always evolving process, and in the case of avoidant attachment presents interesting considerations. This chapter will consider how attachment-based research tools and findings form a useful conceptual bridge to connect researchers and clinicians, particularly when faced with participants or patients with avoidant patterns of attachment.

In writing this, I have the privilege of being able to wear two hats, that of researcher in the field of attachment and of an attachment-based psychoanalytic psychotherapist. As a researcher, I get to use the tools of my trade to investigate attachment and related psychological and physiological phenomena in large samples within the population. As a clinician, it could be argued that I do the same thing, only this time with a sample of one. In an interview, Bowlby explained: "A patient is generalizing from a sample of one; her mother is her sample of one; and she has had that experience" (Hunter, 1994, p. 138).

Both processes enable me to be curious and exploratory, two qualities that are invaluable to attachment, clinical practice, and research. As a researcher, my view is that we are only as good as the tools that we use, and in the "trade" of attachment we have a lot of tools at our disposal. It therefore seems fitting to start this chapter with an overview of attachment-based research tools. As a researcher, I certainly value the use of objective ratings; they provide direct links to the evidence-base and facilitate a common usable language. However, as a psychotherapist, I feel that psychodynamic processes can be lost when using attachment-based research tools in an exclusively quantitative manner. In moving from the research lab to the consulting room, I will consider the question of whether attachment-based research tools can provide valuable "hooks" on which to hang a therapeutic frame for those with avoidant attachment.

Attachment-based research tools

Adult attachment measures, particularly those that are interview-based, have emerged from two distinct research traditions: first, developmental, psychodynamic psychology, with a focus on parenting and predicting intergenerational patterns of attachment quality; and second, social psychology, with an interest in personal adjustment, partner/support relationships and mental health risks (Fraley and Shaver, 2000). The former is typified by the measure of adult attachment that captured the interest of psychoanalysis: the Adult Attachment Interview (AAI) (George et al., 1985), which is a semi-structured interview based upon questions about childhood and early life experience and involves discourse analysis of transcripts. Essentially, the AAI is about how adults have processed their childhood relationships with their parents. The measure focuses on narrative style and uses this to provide a window into an individual's capacity for reflective function. Interviewees' verbatim transcripts are used to classify them as having either a secure, insecure-dismissing or insecure-preoccupied attachment representation. Additionally, there is an overarching classification as to whether the person is "unresolved/disorganised", which is given if the person's reasoning or discourse becomes incoherent in relation to loss or other traumatic events. When an individual does not meet the criteria to be placed in one of the three organised categories, the interview is assigned to the "cannot classify" grouping.

In contrast, the Attachment Style Interview (ASI) (Bifulco *et al.*, 2002) is more aligned with the social psychology approach, and contains questions which are contextualised and support-focused, to assess current interpersonal behaviour and attitudes. The ASI echoes Bowlby's principal concern with observable behaviour rather than speculations about the inner world. Whereas the AAI focuses on the "*way*" of the description, i.e. the *way* the individual describes their relationships with their parents (for example, with idealisation or derogation), the ASI focuses on the "*what*", i.e. *what* is described. This is a key issue that typified the divergence between psychoanalysis and behavioural theories; Bowlby asserted the need for observation in the absence of such approaches, whereas Freud and Klein focused on the internal world of the object. Although Bowlby did see himself as a psychoanalyst, he believed that what happened in a patient's life was as important as unconscious fantasy, and this is reflected in the measurement approach of the ASI with its contextualised focus on support and life events, rooted in the work of Brown and Harris (1978). Conversely, the AAI's focus on "surprising the unconscious" (George *et al.*, 1985) lends itself more towards the observation of the inner, rather than outer, world of the interviewee.

Farnfield (2017) states of the AAI: "What happened (the content) is less important than the coherence of the narrative" (p. 73). The ASI is the other way around. Farnfield also writes:

> The AAI flushes out attempts to exclude information from the self and others. In this regard it is rather like following a Pinter play: the real story is not in the surface speech but the pauses, silences and things people do not say, or say in ways which are designed to disguise their true meaning.
>
> (Ibid., p. 55)

In that case, the ASI could be seen as more like a John Osborne play; the meaning is what is expressed, and all is displayed on stage in the current context of an individual's attachment.

The ASI uses standardised, semi-structured interview questions, and questioning is flexible; additional probing questions can be added when needed to clarify responses and encourage the interviewee to talk, which may be especially important for those with an avoidant attachment style. Probing questions are used to elicit further descriptive material and evidence of behaviour (e.g. "*Can you describe a recent problem that you confided in this person?"*) or frequency (e.g. *"How often do you have arguments or rows?"*) or intensity (e.g. *"How would you feel if your friend moved away to live?"*). The ASI falls into two parts. In the first part respondents are asked questions regarding their relationships with "very close others" and family of origin. Ratings are made along five scales: degree of confiding, active emotional support, positive quality of interaction, negative quality of interaction, and felt attachment in key relationships. This part of the interview largely encompasses behaviour in relationships, with these questions providing both quantified information on the level of support in relationships and descriptive information about the individual's relationships. Therefore, this part of the interview represents the *"how"*, i.e. *how* secure the person's attachment style is (securely attached or mildly, moderately, or markedly insecurely attached).

The second part of the ASI involves exploring global attitudes to others along dimensions of attachment-related anxiety and attachment-related avoidance, with ratings for seven scales of mistrust, constraints on closeness, self-reliance, anger, fear of rejection, fear of separation, and desire for company. This part of the interview represents the *"what"*, i.e. if the person does have an insecure attachment style, then *what* characterises it. There are distinctive patterns of attitudes for each of the four insecure styles. Enmeshed insecure style is characterised by low self-reliance, high desire for company, and fear of separation. Fearful insecure style is characterised by mistrust, constraints on closeness, and fear of rejection. Angry-dismissive insecure style is characterised by mistrust, high self-reliance, and anger. Withdrawn insecure style is typified by constraints on closeness and low desire for company. Those with a secure attachment style present none of these negative attitudinal characteristics and are trusting of others, have low levels of fear and anger in relationships, and have balanced and flexible levels of self-reliance and desire for company. A disorganised attachment style in the ASI can be rated if more than one pattern emerges. Essentially, these ASI attachment attitudes concern intimacy and autonomy which, according to Holmes (2001), are the overall goals of therapy.

Combining these two parts of the ASI gives a person's overall categorisation which, when taking into account all of the insecure styles and combinations, gives thirteen possible overall single attachment styles, e.g. markedly angry-dismissive. To get to this overall category, the ASI is tape-recorded, and then scoring and subsequent classification is undertaken from the recording. The relevant parts of the interview are transcribed onto the scoring schedule, which contains rules to quantify each piece of indicative narrative. Documenting the appropriate pieces of evidence on the scoring schedule to justify the ratings is the essence of the "investigator-based" approach, and this also helps with the inter-rater reliability of the measure. The investigator-based approach requires the interviewer to make use of factual evidence which, according to Bowlby, would be observable in order to make decisions when rating the characteristics of attachment style.

Whereas the AAI is retrospective, the ASI is prospective. It was initially used to identify risk of developing depression. One of the most important findings from initial research using the ASI was the presence of resilience among those with mild levels of either an anxious-insecure or an avoidant-insecure style, whereby the rates of depression were no different from those who were securely attached (Bifulco *et al.*, 2002). Only high levels of insecurity represented a risk pathway for disorder. Therefore, if an individual is insecurely attached, it is important to know *how much*. The different levels of insecurity as assessed by the ASI offer a means of thinking about attachment strategies, particularly how milder levels of each insecure attachment style may be resilient. For example, whereas a markedly withdrawn attachment style may present as cold and non-emotional, mildly withdrawn individuals tend to be rational, practical, and logical.

The ASI also gives a more balanced view of the varieties of avoidant attachment patterns than the AAI, which does not make a basic distinction between fearful and dismissive avoidance (Harris, 2015). Fearful insecure style, as conceptualised by the ASI, embodies a push–pull between anxiety and avoidance. There is anxiety about being hurt or rejected which results in behaviour that is avoidant; these individuals "short-circuit" any potential experiences of vulnerability or distress in relationships (Fraley *et al.*, 2000). The AAI dismissive classification, which represents a highly resilient/self-reliant (like ASI withdrawn) and volatile/prickly/denigrating individual (like ASI angry-dismissive), is also different. Instead of conflating the two, the ASI holds separate categories for withdrawn and angry-dismissive insecure types, which present very differently. Angry-dismissive individuals are characterised by an angry avoidance of relationships and any interaction with others happens through their anger. In contrast, the withdrawn insecure style does not seek interaction with others. This type of insecure avoidance lacks emotionality and is almost defined by what is not there, i.e. no fear, no anxiety and no anger;

these individuals are detached rather than attached. Bearing in mind these differences between the ASI and the AAI, and having worked with both measures, my view is that although both were developed in traditions inspired by Bowlby's attachment theory, to compare the two is like comparing apples and oranges. It is not a dispute about which one is better; rather it is about the choice of tool being aligned with whatever research or clinical aim one has.

From the research lab to the consulting room

In my research using the ASI, I have been mindful of being sensitive and responsive to my research participants and their stories; my participants are people first and foremost, not data. Yet although psychoanalysis and attachment theory have common roots, attachment theory has ended up being far closer to empirical psychology and has thus been more data- and method-bound than meaning-bound over the last two decades. Bowlby rejected the concept of drive theory and the reification of "the unconscious", and he certainly believed that what happened in a patient's life is as important as unconscious fantasy. However, many of attachment theory's significant discoveries can be seen to have been observed "on the couch" as well as in the library and in the lab, and internal working models also provide the foundations for a range of relationships, such as those between patient and clinician (Liotti, 2004), and in my experience, that of researcher and participant.

I first met Anna when she volunteered to be a participant in my postdoctoral research study, which explored the relationship between attachment style and non-suicidal self-injury (Oskis *et al.*, in press). At the time of participating in my research Anna was aged 22. She started self-harming at the age of 15, and these behaviours included cutting, burning, head banging, carving, and scratching her skin with sharp objects. Anna had a myriad of diagnoses at the time of taking part in my study, including schizoaffective disorder, depression, social phobia, and obsessive-compulsive disorder.

According to a standard ASI categorisation, Anna's attachment style was markedly withdrawn. This is an avoidant style characterised by high self-reliance and high constraints on closeness, and there is neither fear of rejection nor high anger. Individuals categorised as having this style have not acquired supportive relationships, evidenced behaviourally by little or no confiding or active emotional support and a "closed" style of relating. The presentation of this style is emotionally detached and non-relational. Before further disentangling this, Anna's overall category would immediately suggest a potential therapeutic difficulty with what Winnicott (1955) would term a necessary regression to dependence as a part of the relational work.

Cundy (2017) states that her initial meeting with a client is semi-structured "letting the patient take the lead but interjecting with questions based on the AAI" (p. 16). Here we see that questions taken from interview-based attachment research tools may provide form and shape to clinical thinking. Putting on my clinician's hat when thinking about Anna's ASI led me to consider that specific scales from Anna's interview could provide valuable "hooks" on which to hang a therapeutic frame for an individual with avoidant attachment. In the ASI, the confiding scale assesses the extent to which the interviewee can talk to the support figure about personal feelings, crises, and emotionally charged topics. Supporting evidence of examples of recent confiding is required. When asked if she confides in her mother, Anna said the following:

> Normally it's all about her and what's happening in her life and that kind of thing. And I would tell her about college, whether I've done well on my coursework or something, whether my class was boring or things like that ... you know, I'll try and tell her something about my day, but then she'll just tell something about what happened at work or something ... I just tend to think that mum's got enough to be getting on with, you know, I'm not going to give her more.

Anna's lack of confiding in her mother, and conversely her mother's confiding in *her* suggests, in Winnicottian terms, that her mother may not have provided a "good enough" holding environment in her early years. Anna's personality would therefore have been built on the basis of reactions to the environmental impingement of an inconsistent, depressed mother who is preoccupied with her own needs (Winnicott, 1960a). A prominent psychodynamic hypothesis of self-injury concerns rage towards the self or the "bad" internal object, echoing Winnicott's (1960a, p. 45) view of the "psyche indwelling in the soma". Freud (1920) and Klein (1935) suggest these individuals identify with the lost object and attack that object within themselves, such that killing the self also is, in fantasy, conceived of as killing someone who has caused great hurt. The desire to rid the self of the "bad" may go some way to account for there being no physical pain when inflicting self-harm. A further psychodynamic view, which resonates with attachment theory, is proposed by

Favazza and Conterio (1989) who suggest that deliberate self-injury is more likely to occur in response to separation. This links to an issue of parentification and role-reversal; as we see here, it is Anna's mother who confides in *her*, effectively abandoning her own maternal role.

Interestingly, the interview questions regarding confiding in her father revealed powerful Oedipal dynamic forces at play in Anna's home life. Speaking of a recent example of confiding in her father, Anna said:

> I spoke to him over the last few months about how I think it's unfair that mum takes him away all the time, and how mum's always saying that he needs to sleep when he comes home, and it's a bit hypocritical when she gets him to take her out, when he needs his rest, and she says that. That kind of thing … He feels the same way. But it did kind of make me wish that he'd kind of take a step to kind of you know, stand up to mum and make sure that he does get a rest when he needs to.

Anna revisited this idea later in her interview when talking about the negative interaction with her mother. This scale explores the extent to which time spent together is characterised by a negative tone, and the intensity of any tension and rows. She said:

> Um, I'd say there's a bit of tension about my dad, because I'm very close with my dad, I certainly get on with him better than I do with my mum. But whenever he comes home, mum kind of gets him to take her out, go away for the night, so I barely get to see him, which is kind of frustrating. I have kind of, kind of in a passive aggressive way I guess, just made sarcastic comments whenever they go out or whatever, and I think she has picked up on that, because the other weekend, she allowed me and my dad to go for lunch together, which was, you know, something. So that was nice. But I never sort of confronted her properly about it.

The Oedipal myth communicates "the child's need to learn about generational difference, to manage hostility and jealousy, and the seductiveness of overly close relationships between parent and child" (Anderson *et al.*, 2012, p. 132). These are hidden or unacknowledged aspects of relationships and/or experience that lie within the family. Therefore, the ASI could potentially be used to uncover these aspects of relationships which, in turn, would be likely to be re-enacted in a therapeutic relationship.

The afore-mentioned scales of the ASI elicit examples of the interviewee's actual support-seeking behaviour. As stated above, the second part of the interview concerns attitudes towards support seeking. These largely concern closeness and distance in relationships. In Anna's ASI, two scales concerning distance in relationships were present at marked levels, and both could have potential implications for therapy. These were mistrust and constraints on closeness. Mistrust is the extent to which the interviewee lacks trust in people close to him/her as well as outsiders, and is suspicious of their motives and behaviour. Regarding mistrust, Anna said:

> Well my problem is that um, it takes me a long time to trust people. So, because I'm still in therapy now, and I've been with the therapist that I'm with now for like two years, and it's taken me about a year to get to the point where I can even start anything with her.

Cooper (1987) states that there are predictable reactions that will arise in the transference when a patient holds certain beliefs or attitudes. For example, mistrust may be re-enacted in the consulting room possibly as mistrust of the analyst's capacity to tolerate "bad" or hateful feelings. Looking at this from an attachment-based viewpoint fits with Bowlby's therapeutic approach which, in the words of Ezquerro (2015), "went beyond transference interpretations. He put a greater emphasis on the need that patients often have to perceive the therapist as a trusted companion who provides support, encouragement, sympathy and, on occasion, guidance" (p. 168).

The constraints on closeness scale of the ASI explores the psychological blockages inhibiting the development or maintenance of close confiding relationships and care eliciting. Barriers within the individual to achieving closeness and seeking help are explored. Anna said of her college friend: "I would never give her reason to think things aren't right." She then said generally of people:

> Yeah, um I mean, I normally find people thinking they're close to me, when they're not, so I kind of give them enough for them to think that they're close, but I'm always miles away … I don't really tell them much about myself, and just let it be one way, them telling me about themselves and not really giving much away about myself.… I'm just generally uncomfortable in social interactions. I mean, I think it's partly because I don't have much of a sense of a

self-concept in a sense. I don't really have a strong sense of self. I tend to adapt myself according to the people that I am around and what they need me to be.

Her response in this part of the interview suggests a potential issue of a "false self" defence (Winnicott, 1960b), which may be important as therapy progresses, and also highlights the importance of Anna's stage of first object-relationships, and the likelihood of Anna's mother as a not "good-enough" mother in this stage of development. Also, in relation to the constraints on closeness scale Anna said: "I don't like seeking help, so it just comes down to me just finding a way to cope and just, you know, getting on with it."

Moreover, in relation to self-reliance, a high rating for which is key to the ASI withdrawn category, Anna said:

I'm very determined so I'll tend to ask people their opinions and then kind of go with what I want anyway. My mum always says that, you know, if I ask for advice on something, I'll probably go with the opposite of what she says anyway, and that kind of thing.

The verbatim from this ASI scale shows how Anna appears to protest for her autonomy, which from a Winnicottian perspective may be about her protest for separation from her mother, with whom she is symbiotically fused. In other words, by attacking and destroying her mother Anna can forge a separation with her (Winnicott, 1969).

Conclusion

The availability of research-based assessment tools to practitioners, such as the ASI, creates one type of bridge between research and clinical practice. This conforms to a model of research utilisation termed "embedded research", described by Bullock (2006) as: "Where research-informed practice is achieved indirectly by embedding research findings and methods in the systems and processes of social care, such as standards, policies, procedures and tools" (p. 21).

Harris talks about her experience of using the ASI in her own research and the links she has made to her clinical practice. In particular, she highlights a consideration prompted by responses of participants to the ASI active emotional support scale, saying:

> I have found they have alerted me to ways in which my own behaviour in sessions might negatively impact on my clients. First by hearing so many different examples of feeling "let down" I have been sensitised to how easily remarks can be misinterpreted and this has increased my determination to avoid any comment that might be seen as laying any blame at the client's door.
>
> (Harris, 2015, p. 183)

The naturalistic accounts of relationships outside the consulting room provided by a tool such as the ASI may offer an insight into the strategies of those with avoidant insecure attachment styles, specifically for the withdrawn types who tend to minimise the role of support in relationships, or for angry-dismissive styles whose tendency is to perceive remarks as attacks on the self. If the tendency of these individuals is to avoid then, particularly in the initial stages of therapy, it may be useful to find "another way in"; using a more structured and boundaried interview like the ASI, as opposed to a spontaneous and open format, may be fruitful. Hill and Dallos (2012) reached a similar conclusion after using the Biographical Narrative Interview Method in their research study, commenting that "this way of telling their story allowed them to remain emotionally distanced" (2012, p. 469).

The saying goes that "if the only tool you have is a hammer, you'll treat everything as a nail". However, in the spirit of this chapter perhaps it could be modified along the lines "if the only tool you have is an ASI or AAI, you'll treat everything as a category". In my clinical experience, this is not necessarily true. Using attachment-based research tools gives us so much more than a categorisation. If research using the ASI tells me that there is evidence of links between constraints on closeness and self-harming behaviours (Oskis *et al.*, in press) or alexithymia (Oskis *et al.*, 2013), then for a client who presents with these issues I can use the ASI to inform my thinking and help me generate meaningful questions and areas of exploration during the therapy. But this is not my only tool in the consulting room. For example, paying attention to the client's attitude to boundaries, how the client engages with me, and my own counter-transference are just as important.

> The truth is that neither class of data [clinical nor research observations] is intrinsically better than the other. Each is relevant to the problems with which psychoanalysis grapples and the contribution made by each is likely to be enhanced when seen in conjunction

with the contribution made by the other. Binocular vision is better than the vision of either eye used separately.

(Bowlby, 1969/1991, p. 6)

I do not avoid the bridge between research and clinical practice. In fact, I walk across it regularly.

References

Anderson, J., Hurst, M., Marques, A., Millar, D., Moya, S., Pover, L., and Stewart, S. (2012). Understanding suicidal behaviour in young people referred to specialist CAMHS: A qualitative psychoanalytic clinical research project. *Journal of Child Psychotherapy, 38*(2), 130–153.

Bifulco, A., Moran, P. M., Ball, C., and Bernazzani, O. (2002). Adult attachment style. I: Its relationship to clinical depression. *Social Psychiatry and Psychiatric Epidemiology, 37*(2), 50–59.

Bowlby, J. (1969). *Attachment and Loss: Volume 1: Attachment*. London: Hogarth Press/Institute of Psycho-Analysis. Reprinted 1991. London: Penguin.

Bowlby, J. (1998). *A Secure Base: Clinical Applications of Attachment Theory*. London: Routledge.

Brown, G. W. and Harris, T. (1978). Social origins of depression: A reply. *Psychological Medicine, 8*(4), 577–588.

Bullock, R. (2006). The dissemination of research findings in Children's Services: Issues and strategies. *Adoption & Fostering, 30*(1), 18–28.

Cooper, A. M. (1987). Changes in psychoanalytic ideas: Transference interpretation. *Journal of the American Psychoanalytic Association, 35*(1), 77–98.

Cundy, L. (2017). Fear of abandonment and angry protest: Understanding and working with anxiously attached clients. In: L. Cundy (ed.), *Anxiously Attached: Understanding and Working with Preoccupied Attachment* (pp. 1–30). London: Karnac.

Ezquerro, A. (2015). John Bowlby: The timeless supervisor. *Attachment, 9*(2), 165–175.

Farnfield, S. (2017). The Adult Attachment Interview: Information processing and the distinguishing features of preoccupied attachment – or: What has attachment theory ever done for us? In: L. Cundy (ed.), *Anxiously Attached: Understanding and Working with Preoccupied Attachment* (pp. 43–67). London: Karnac, 2017.

Favazza, A. R. and Conterio, K. (1989). Female habitual self mutilators. *Acta Psychiatrica Scandinavica, 79*(3), 283–289.

Fraley, R. C. and Shaver, P. R. (2000). Adult romantic attachment: Theoretical developments, emerging controversies, and unanswered questions. *Review of General Psychology, 4*(2), 132–154.

Fraley, R. C., Garner, J. P., and Shaver, P. R. (2000). Adult attachment and the defensive regulation of attention and memory: Examining the role of preemptive and postemptive defensive processes. *Journal of Personality and Social Psychology, 79*(5), 816–826.
Freud, S. (1920). Beyond the pleasure principle. *Standard Edition, 18,* 1–64.
George, C., Kaplan, N., and Main, M. (1985). The Berkeley Adult Attachment Interview. Unpublished manuscript, University of California, Berkeley, CA.
Harris, T. (2015). Not by a fence: A reminder for attachment psychotherapists about the importance of the client's current external social network. *Attachment: New Directions in Relational Psychoanalysis and Psychotherapy, 9*(2), 176–187.
Hill, K. and Dallos, R. (2012). Young people's stories of self-harm: A narrative study. *Clinical Child Psychology and Psychiatry, 17*(3), 459–475.
Holmes, J. (2001). *The Search for the Secure Base: Attachment Theory and Psychotherapy.* London: Routledge.
Hunter, V. (1994). *Psychoanalysts Talk.* New York: Guilford Press.
Klein, M. (1935). A contribution to the psychogenesis of manic-depressive states. *International Journal of Psycho-Analysis, 16,* 145–174.
Liotti, G. (2004). Trauma, dissociation, and disorganized attachment: Three strands of a single braid. *Psychotherapy: Theory, Research, Practice, Training, 41*(4), 472.
Oskis, A. and Borrill J. Using the Attachment Style Interview to explore self-harm in men: A tool to bridge research and clinical practice. Under review. *International Journal of Multidisciplinary Trauma Studies.*
Oskis, A., Loveday, C., Hucklebridge, F., Bifulco, A., Jacobs, C., and Clow, A. (2013). Understanding alexithymia in female adolescents: The role of attachment style. *Personality and Individual Differences, 54*(1), 97–102.
Oskis, A., Borrill, J., and Bifulco, A. Attachment style and alexithymia as predictors of self-harm in young adults: A pilot study. In press. *International Journal of Multidisciplinary Trauma Studies.*
Winnicott, D. W. (1955). Metapsychological and clinical aspects of regression within the psycho-analytical set-up. *International Journal of Psycho-Analysis, 36*(1), 16–26.
Winnicott, D. W. (1960a). The theory of the parent–infant relationship. *International Journal of Psycho-Analysis, 41*(6), 585–595.
Winnicott, D. W. (1960b). Ego distortion in terms of true and false self. In: D. W. Winnicott (1965), *The Maturational Processes and the Facilitating Environment* (pp. 140–152). London: Hogarth Press.
Winnicott, D. W. (1969). The use of an object and relating through identifications. *International Journal of Psycho-Analysis, 50*(4), 711–716.

CHAPTER THREE

Avoidant people in relationships: why would they bother? How do partners fare?

Anne Power

> ... someone who is readily plunged into prolonged moods of hopelessness and helplessness has been exposed repeatedly during infancy and childhood to situations in which his attempts to influence his parents to give him more time, affection and understanding have met with nothing but rebuff and punishment.
>
> (Bowlby, 1979, p. 158)

Introductory anecdote

I was reflecting with a colleague on my work with Mike,[1] a man with an avoidant attachment strategy, and I was describing to her how low-key and repetitive sessions could feel. Mike had come to therapy when, to his complete surprise, he had started having serious panic attacks. In sessions I was often led into being more active than I felt was wise and I knew I was making myself too busy trying to tempt him to join me in exploration. I wondered what I might be missing in my zeal to find out what was going on in Mike and I came up with the idea that perhaps I ought to be wearing my distance glasses when working with him. I explained to my colleague that I needed spectacles for driving and television but usually I got by well enough with the middle distance so I had never wanted or needed to wear glasses for one-to-one interactions. But I was anxious that I was not detecting enough of Mike, worried that I was missing what he needed me to catch. I thought, "If I could only see him better I would be able to reach him."

My colleague paused and then we both smiled as I could suddenly see that I had been applying a practical solution to a psychic need. Mike was transmitting a message of "Please see me" because this was someone who had never felt seen, who tried very hard not to be seen for who he was, who had not yet been able to risk being deeply seen. What he needed from me was not to put on a pair of spectacles, but to communicate that I saw his longing and his predicament. I think that a dynamic like this can often occur with avoidant clients because their longing to be seen has been so well disguised that it can reach us in unexpected ways.

In this chapter I will first outline the paradoxical experience of being avoidantly attached, then look at the couple experience, and finally think about how we work – with couples and with individuals but always holding the couple in mind.

The avoidant core defence – its pain and its importance

Avoidant individuals have had to adapt to caregivers who were non-reciprocal, dismissive, or disparaging, so that they felt needed rather than wanted, and this is the core attachment wound behind their guarded defences. As children they learned to be both self-soothing and self-stimulating, a pattern which makes adult couple relationships difficult.

One writer who presents a very clear and compassionate understanding of the avoidant person in relationships is Tatkin. He stresses how avoidance is an adaptation, and the greater the adaptation the more the person appears not to need others. He offers an interesting hypothesis: "The avoidant's pseudosecurity is rooted in a fantasy of omnipresence and permanence. This fantasy allows the avoidant to spend extended time away from the primary figure" (Tatkin, 2009a, p. 13).

Whereas the preoccupied person expects abandonment, the avoidant assumes permanence but with neglect. Avoidant defences can make an individual quite emotionally blind to how his or her partner is feeling. It is often a complete surprise if an ambivalent partner gets fed up and finally leaves, so complete was their assumption that the other would continue to be there pestering for attention.

Castellano and colleagues offer a similarly poignant description of the handicap dismissing clients bring to relationships. They stress how a pattern of conflict avoidance can rob a couple of intimacy.

> In these circumstances, relationships lose their vitality, as the partners become fixed in a pattern of relating aimed at minimising or passively tolerating ruptures, because they can neither signal their distress ... nor confront the ruptures and their emotions when they occur.
> (Castellano *et al.*, 2014, p. 72)

Given their discomfort with closeness, we might wonder why avoidant individuals bother with relationships. The answer to this is clear in Bowlby's observation that human beings are shaped by attachment needs; avoidant/dismissing people have just as much *need* for proximity and responsiveness, but they have a particular way of managing closeness and minimising attachment emotions. These strategies were learned in response to a rejecting or intrusive caregiver; avoidance is a compromise strategy for achieving a measure of proximity to a neglectful caregiver. In these families the best chance of care came to children who could defensively exclude their desire for closeness and comfort. This is the backstory of our dismissing patients who are over-succinct and do not readily collaborate. These individuals find intimacy with others difficult and, as Wallin puts it, "they are no more intimate with themselves" (Wallin, 2007, p. 211). This distance from the self has to be maintained for the avoidant person to feel safe and, sitting opposite us, such a client may be unconsciously thinking: "If I allow myself to feel this then I lose my most important connection ... to my internal minimiser who reliably manages everything for me".

As avoidant clients are so practised at hiding vulnerability we have to be both vigilant and lucky to spot these feelings, which show up in the laboratory setting when heart rate and cortisol are checked. This desperation to identify the feelings being evaded was what lay behind my idea of needing to wear spectacles to work with Mike. I was aware that the process by which internal working models impact is automatic, reflexive, and very fast, and I wanted extra strong vision to catch these movements.

It seems that as soon as there is a murmur of a sad feeling Mike has an internal panic and the offending vulnerability is brusquely swept aside. On the surface there is barely a ripple – yet there *is* a trace of a ripple and I am slowly getting better at spotting this and intervening with a description of these signs of his struggle. It is this minimising of affect, so hard to see, which is producing in me the idea that I need to wear spectacles. Now and again a new sliver of emotional experience is described between us and owned by Mike, and I am trying to recruit him into the exploration by asking how he thinks we are doing in this tracking task. I am aiming not so much to coax him to increased openness with himself as to engage him in researching his resistance. What is he getting from things as they are? What concept does he have of where his feelings are and how they are impacting? What somatic clues can he begin to track?

Mike sometimes surprises me with his powerful use of imagery and in the following observation he conveys how fully adapted he is to living within the limitations of an avoidant defence. He acknowledges that he repeatedly steps away from my various invitations to stay with a vulnerable feeling and then he comes up with a driving metaphor to explain why he might be happy as he his, keeping his feelings in their boxes. He said:

> It's as though there is an imbalance in the steering of my car – every time I break we veer off to the right, but it's not actually a problem because I know it always does that and so I've learnt to adjust my driving.

He is making a good case – with defences as comfortable as this why would he want to change them? At that point he was forgetting the panic attacks which brought him and which disappeared soon after starting therapy.

To further understand the dismissing dilemma we can distinguish between the impact of mild distress and that of serious attachment-related stress. When an avoidant person feels mild distress (and this is not attachment related) he or she can seek care and can also give it. They may enjoy giving "instrumental" care. However, when issues of attachment and loss become intense, then avoidant defences will be switched on. If a partner needs support at such a moment it cannot be forthcoming and they will be dismayed to find that their avoidant partner withdraws at precisely the moment that care is needed and hoped for. If distress were to become very severe then these distancing, deactivating strategies will in turn break down and then the avoidant person's vulnerability may be painfully over-exposed. This is one way of understanding the brittleness of the False Self: if it does begin to crack there may be a dramatic loss of function before, we hope, recovery to a more sustainable and integrated experience of self. Winnicott (1960) counsels that if we are not prepared for a very high degree of regression and dependence we should not take on patients with this kind of defence.

Bartholomew and Horowitz looked at the internal working models involved in dismissing strategies to propose a distinction between different types of avoidance. They write of the dismissing avoidant group as having "a sense of love-worthiness combined with a negative disposition towards other people" (Bartholomew and Horowitz, 1991, p. 227). The fearful avoidant group are described as having "a sense of unworthiness (unlovability) combined with an expectation that others will be negatively disposed (untrustworthy and rejecting)" (ibid.). Many therapists find that these sub-groups describe the felt sense they have in the room with clients while others are not convinced by the portrayal of dismissing clients as having a positive view of self.

Mikulincer (1995) argues that the apparent self-confidence and arrogance of avoidant people does not reflect genuine good feeling about the self, but self-esteem so fragile that flaws cannot be tolerated. The self is idealised as a defence against the fear that one is not perfect. We might see the fearful avoidant as having the opposite defence: they denigrate the self ("I know I'm rubbish") to deflect other people's disappointment. Both groups are trying to protect themselves against rejection but Bartholomew and Horowitz's theory seems not to offer the dismissing group the same degree of empathy. An observation from Clulow seems to apply well here: "Idealisation (and its related opposite, denigration) represents an attempt to enshrine a relational image and protect it against experiences and feelings that might challenge it" (1998, p. 458).

An alternative categorisation is offered by Crittenden (1995). She distinguishes between different types of parental neglect; the strategy developed to cope with an intrusive mother differs from that evolved to deal with a withdrawing caregiver. In the case of intrusion, the child learns to down-regulate and to behave in cool, polite, and formal ways as the best method for discouraging attention. Where a mother withdraws, the child may display falsely positive feelings to signal that all is fine and no demands will be made. When an adult client performs in this upbeat way we tend to feel distanced and perhaps bored.

Wallin (2007) also offers us a way of distinguishing between different styles of avoidance. He first describes the defensive devaluing approach where life is managed through an illusion of specialness, like a starving man who says the food isn't worth eating. Second, is the idealising strategy adopted by those who have learned that by making the parent feel special, they could themselves get a bit of that feeling. In therapy these patients appear more involved but they are in fact controlling the distance. Third, a controlling group are often seen as "obsessive". Like all avoidant people, they cope by keeping feelings at bay, but in addition this group resist being controlled by others and seek to be the ones in power; hence, in therapy, they may be focused on a power struggle.

My client Fiona might be understood as having the defensive devaluing profile described by Wallin; there is something in her manner that is more defiant, arrogant, and aloof than that of Mike. From the point of view of Bartholomew and Horowitz (1991) she would be thought of as dismissing. However, in my view this would be misleading as she does not feel good about herself, though in her defended modes she would claim otherwise. Fiona was very reluctant to be in therapy but a thoughtful GP sent her when a succession of symptoms was hard to treat and eventually her blood pressure would not respond sufficiently to medication. She drinks heavily with colleagues and I sense she uses alcohol to buttress her avoidant defences. I also sense that she uses sexual relating as a way to keep feelings and intimacy at bay. When I observed that it might be hard for Fiona to come to sessions because she has found it very difficult to let people care for her, she had a very quick reply which skilfully put me right back in my place on the other side of the room: "No, I've got no problem with coming here – this is *self*-care, I'm looking after myself by paying to see you".

In the room I can sometimes track Fiona's anxiety in her breathing but I am still trying to engage her in curiosity about her body. Whether by tone or by turn of phrase she is skilled at deflecting and dismissing my enquiries. On the other hand, she has found a way to let me in: she has surprised me by bringing very interesting dreams. Recently she told me of a dream which focused on a kindly but severe teacher in a basement classroom. My room is a basement but she had no ideas at all about possible associations and preferred to disparage her own dream rather than allow that it could be speaking of me. I take the dream as a sign that she is beginning to let the process be important, but her conscious response is a sign that it is too soon for us to speak of this openly. Meanwhile, I believe it is important to show that I hear her doubts about the process – that I hear them and am not bothered by them. I think this is helping us build a viable working alliance. I also know that just to accommodate to her allergy against intimacy would be to humour the False Self, so it is essential that I also challenge her. I think Fiona embodies the dilemma described by Winnicott's comments about the False Self; both she and I perhaps dread the degree of falling apart that may lie ahead.

Where Mike might be understood in Crittenden's terms as the cool, polite child of an intrusive mother, another client, Cheryl, fits Crittenden's other category: the falsely positive child of a withdrawing mother. Cheryl learned to signal strongly that she is absolutely *fine* and there is no risk of her asking for help. Like Mike, these clients are polite and superficially can appear warm, but the self is even more armoured by virtue of the need to relentlessly transmit a message of cheeriness. Cheryl was very able and very charming but after our first break she did not return or make any closing communication. Afterwards, I concluded that I had been misled, during our eight weeks of work, into thinking we were making a connection and I had greatly underestimated her level of avoidance. I think that for her to return after the break would have felt to her dismissing self that she was showing neediness. Her arrival in therapy had been a huge step taken at a point of great anxiety as to whether to take things forward with her girlfriend; returning after a break might have been even harder than presenting for help in the first instance. Possibly, if I had anticipated that dilemma more fully it could have been contained. The picture she had given me of her relationship with her girlfriend might have alerted me; she had no concept of looking for support for herself, the relationship was something of a puzzle to her, she picked her way as though through a dangerous landscape, trying to behave in ways that she imagined her partner wanted, trying to avoid the landmines and to learn by rote from her girlfriend's criticisms.

Culture

If we work with a multicultural client group it could be helpful to understand how different cultures shape childcare and thus impact on attachment. Studies of different social groups have shown that while attachment stands up well as a construct across variations in culture, localised child rearing practices do leave their mark (Harwood *et al.*, 1995; van IJzendoorn and Kroonenberg, 1988). For this reason a low level of avoidance may be "culturally syntonic" in some sub- cultures such as boarding school and British establishment institutions, which have remained infused with that ethos of self-sufficiency. In these settings, avoidance is not necessarily a problem. In Britain, the upper classes have maintained a tradition of sending young children to boarding school, which tends to confirm and amplify the avoidant pattern that many of these children will already have evolved at home. In this way the wider social group supports families who under-respond to empathy and celebrate early independence (Duffell, 2000; Power, 2013; Schaverien, 2015). When children with insecure patterns are sent away young they may not be able to benefit from the apparent privileges of boarding school and those with avoidant patterns are equipped by their reduced empathy and distance to become bullies. Although their bullying is often targeted at children with more preoccupied patterns whose vulnerabilities are most visible, the outcome is as bad for the bullies as for those they menace.

When a boarding school survivor with a dismissing pattern of attachment wants to settle down in a long-term relationship, his or her avoidant strategies may become problematic and not uncommonly partners may demand that they go into therapy. With such clients the transference is likely to hold us at a distance. If the client's own avoidant pattern also features the arrogance and sense of entitlement bequeathed by their education, then the combination will be very powerful. This will impact on us as therapists according to our own backgrounds: those from similar backgrounds may feel pulled to indicate in some way that they are also of the in-group while those from backgrounds with less status may feel alienated. Either way the therapy is undermined.

Like the boarding school experience, the new digital climate may favour those with avoidant patterns because these impersonalised, mechanised forms of interacting support the avoidant person's reliance on distance. As technology makes it easier to entertain a long-distance relationship, more people are choosing to pair with a partner in another country or even another continent. The digital world also provides escape for those with partners living closer to home, or in the same home: keeping up with work and social media can be a handy excuse for keeping intimacy at bay, while addiction to porn is another risk.

On the other hand, there are aspects of the digital age that can be especially stressful for avoidant individuals; technology can make it harder for them to sustain a comfortable distance. Typically, a more preoccupied partner will want to use technology to increase access. They may text several times a day, and if they do text they will expect a reply. They may long for their partner to sign up to an app that allows them to be tracked and located at all times, or at least detect the whereabouts of the mobile phone. These demands for access and response tend to be disturbing for an avoidant person. They may be able to resist the pressures to communicate but resistance costs them energy and presents them with unwelcome emotional tasks: holding the other at bay, holding one's own irritated response at bay. Tatkin (2009a) reflects on the extra effort that avoidant people have to make in a relationship. As part of a couple they tend to feel intruded on simply by the approach of their partner; if they are in a self-regulating state when a partner initiates contact they will begrudge the "effort" needed to make a response. Tatkin suggests that this rejection of the partner's approach is "not so much antisocial as energy conserving" (2009a, p. 11). They are reluctant to connect because their internal working models tell them that the approach of another signals demands, and because of the energy they have to muster for the transition out of the mildly dissociative state into a more active False Self mode: "The auto-regulatory state is dissociative, energy conserving and non-interactive. On a neurological level, brain metabolism is low, as is demand for the brain's resources" (ibid., p. 12).

What happens in relationships

A relationship potentially supplies wonderful containment for both partners, but the catch is that it may also evoke feelings too powerful or toxic to be contained. This can be a painful paradox for any insecurely attached partners, but avoidant individuals are particularly challenged because they are often in denial that there is a problem that needs to be addressed. My reflections here on couple dynamics could apply to any pairs who aspire to monogamy – whether same sex or heterosexual couples. Polyamory raises other considerations. Bowlby asserted, and research affirms, that attachment needs are a lifelong driver. In adults, this longing is most visible in our search for a mate and the drive to become part of a couple is the search for a secure base, for a relationship that can function as a container. Hence, we see proximity seeking between partners when distressed (most poignantly the telephone calls from the doomed planes on 9/11), and protest at separation (for example, divorce or death).

As in other attachment relationships, security is measured in terms of how responsive and accessible the partners are and the degree to which the relationship is experienced as a secure base. A secure partnership will have some reciprocity and flexibility in using each other as support; the fit between each partner's care-giving and care-seeking styles will be important (Crowell and Treboux, 2001).

> Generally it can be said that a person's ability to pick up and understand the attachment signals from a partner, and to reflect on his or her mental states, are essential prerequisites for developing a solid and emotionally involved relationship.
> (Castellano *et al.*, 2014, p. xvii)

The adult pair bond is usually understood as based around three elements: attachment, care-giving, and sexuality. Some couples achieve a balance between these three, but many couples fall into a pattern of imbalance and often this can become a source of unhappiness, with either partner describing too much or too little attachment, caring, or sex. An avoidant partner might typically use sex or care-giving in a compulsive way which helps divert him or her from his/her attachment needs.

All individuals have to manage their conflicting needs for connection and autonomy, and all romantic partnerships have to try to manage this tension in a way that works well enough for both partners. Where one partner is avoidant, he or she is likely to want more space while the other partner wants more closeness. The avoidant person's need for distance from a partner is linked to their need to maintain distance from the self. Because these individuals lack capacity to regulate feelings they rely largely on banning their emotions. Distancing and withdrawal from a relationship may be actual (staying late at work, leaving the relationship) or more psychological, simply being tuned out most of the time, physically present but emotionally absent.

While a very avoidant person might find him- or herself married, when things became difficult the likely solution would probably be withdrawal and denial. Therapy would not be a first choice and in my experience the most highly avoidant individuals are more likely to come to therapy as half of a couple, often if the more ambivalent partner has already given an ultimatum with a threat of leaving.

The statistics are not propitious for people with dismissing patterns. Individuals measured as avoidant reported relationships as low in intimacy, low in mutual disclosure, and low in effective problem-solving communication (Collins and Feeney, 2004). Researchers have also found:

- lower levels of receptivity, gazing, facial and vocal pleasantness, interest and attentiveness (Guerrero, 1996);
- less capacity to read a partner's feelings (Feeney *et al.*, 1994);
- less enjoyment in their interactions (Tidwell *et al.*, 1996).

This lack of pleasure in relationships is significant because it indicates the low reward for avoidant people in relationships, and thus how the defensive pattern becomes reinforced. In addition, individuals with this pattern will tend to evade conflict and have low expectations of a partner and a relationship. These factors may contribute to relationship longevity, if not satisfaction.

Care-giving and care-seeking are both vital skills in a couple relationship and both are difficult for someone with avoidant patterns. Their defences prompt them to miscue when they need care and to withdraw at the point a partner needs it. Where a more secure individual has the resources to allow themselves to become involved in the other's distress – to listen, to offer help – a more avoidant individual will tend to be threatened by the partner's distress and the implicit or explicit request for care-giving. Reibstein describes the rigidity of insecure relationships and how defensive strategies get in the way of a compassionate connection: "Protecting the self becomes the primary objective and overrides the ability to respond to or be empathic to the partner" (1998, p. 353).

These misattunements are specific to attachment experience. Provided he or she is not under stress and a partner only needs *instrumental* help, an avoidant person can do reasonably well at care-giving (Simpson *et al.*, 2007). If the partner's distress is about the relationship or a joint distress (such as loss of a pregnancy), dismissing people find it particularly hard to give comfort because at that moment they need to regulate themselves by withdrawing. Castellano and colleagues describe the mechanical quality to care-giving: "Their need to minimise the significance of attachment-related feelings diverts their attention from the needs of their partner, and they may only offer support to avoid repercussions or to eliminate a source of nuisance" (Castellano *et al.*, 2014, p. 47).

Choosing a mate and then transitioning to attachment

Research cannot predict mate selection based on attachment profile but everyday observation suggests that secure individuals are more likely to pair with secure mates and insecure people with insecure partners. We might imagine that a secure individual would be unlikely to stay long with a very avoidant person because they would feel disappointed by the low level of intimacy and be more able to move on. We also know that insecure attachment in an individual will naturally bleed into any couple relationship; Jung describes this neatly as well as indicating the opportunity for growth that couple relationships can offer: "This disunity with oneself begets discontent, and since one is not conscious of the real state of things one generally projects the reason for it upon one's partner. A critical atmosphere thus develops, the necessary prelude to conscious realization" (Jung, 2014, p. 194).

Among insecure people, a common pairing is between one avoidant and one ambivalent partner. This relationship may be unsatisfying for both parties but it is often enduring, especially in a heterosexual pair when the avoidant partner is male and the preoccupied one is a woman (Kirkpatrick and Davis, 1994). In this kind of pairing, the individual who has been socialised to nurture relationships (the woman) is also the one who fears abandonment and thus has a dual motivation to keep the relationship going. Another aspect of this traditional separation of roles is that women are expected to carry men's denied dependency needs, and men to carry the independence disavowed by women. When the preoccupied partner is the man he will usually have less skill in nurturing the relationship, and perhaps be less willing to take on dependency that is denied by his dismissing partner.

Attachment theory can explain this bond in terms of a fit between two sets of internal working models. Each partner finds something familiar which meets their expectations: preoccupied people expect partners to have low interest and attention; dismissing people expect partners to be overly demanding. Psychodynamic thinking would suggest an additional reason: we fall in love with people who carry a disavowed part of the self – this is the projected fit. For the avoidant partner, the ambivalent is carrying his or her vulnerability and longing for closeness; for the preoccupied person the avoidant is carrying his or her independence.

Dismissing individuals are sometimes attracted to people like themselves, and an avoidant/avoidant couple could be comfortable together until one or both of them has a level of distress which cannot be stemmed by their combined pattern of minimising. At that point the relationship could break down very fast as they are both inclined to withdraw. Solomon and Tatkin (2011) describe pseudo-secure relationships in which a bond between two avoidant people can look quite companionable but actually lacks any depth and intimacy and cannot survive challenges. Partners do not notice the complexity of the other, any novelty would threaten the false sense of security, and so curiosity is shut down. Tatkin argues that these avoidantly attached partners value continual but *implicit* proximity to their primary attachment figure but without the challenge of real *emotional* proximity which always threatens to interfere with the avoidant person's strategy of autoregulation. He describes this self-regulation through distance as "addiction to alone time" (Tatkin, 2009b). These are brittle relationships that lack the capacity to repair ruptures, yet it seems important to recognise that many avoidant people may count this kind of domestic alliance as a good enough outcome.

Finally, as Holmes (2001) commented, a very avoidant individual might possibly form a bond with someone with a disorganised attachment, as they would be equipped to screen out the extreme oscillations in their partner's mood, and the chaotic, uncontained partner would be carrying the intense feelings that the avoidant person most fears knowing in themselves. I recall a case that powerfully illustrates this point. I started seeing a woman in her thirties who I sensed was very disorganised; every factor in her story and how we interacted in the room suggested this, yet she told me she had just come out of a nine-year relationship. For some sessions I could not make sense of this and had to sit with the incongruity, and only some weeks later did I learn that her former partner had been smoking marijuana all day, every day. Whatever his own attachment pattern the use of this drug would appear to have rendered him avoidant in terms of his engagement with her. Another individual appeared to be in a similar kind of arrangement. In this case the avoidant person was my client, with cool, polite traits; all that I heard of his partner, including her early trauma, indicated a disorganised attachment pattern. My client was able to enhance his avoidant defence by being frequently absent on business trips. What I did not realise for a long time was that he was further supporting his detachment through a harmful level of drinking. As with the partner who was using marijuana, the dismissing partner seemed to be using a drug to exaggerate his avoidant strategy in order to be able to stay with a very disorganised, chaotic spouse.

In the West, for the last century, falling in love has been the dominant method of mate selection. This method relies on unconscious process rather than rational choice. Arguably, internet dating sites along with a growth in faith groups who use arranged marriage may mean we are slightly increasing our reliance on logic and decreasing our belief in the magic of love. This could be a very interesting cultural development, possibly involving losses and gains (Power, 2018, in press).

When partner choice is made through falling in love we might see three components:

1. **The conscious bit**: "We both love sailing and we laugh at the same films." Or, "I respected her work ethic." Or, "We share the same family values." This is generally the aspect that the couple themselves emphasise but which may, by far, have the least impact on the outcome of the relationship.
2. **The half-conscious social dictates**: the impact of social environment; for example, having similar social class, ethnicity, education, or choosing to break away from own background. The very need to get settled at all may come from this cultural pressure.
3. **The unconscious dynamics**:
    a choosing someone we hope will complete us;
    b choosing someone who approximates (or sometimes is the mirror of) a family member.

This latter factor, the unconscious dynamic fit, is usually the least recognised by the couple but the most influential in how their relationship develops. Part of the unconscious fit is the *hope* that in this new relationship the hurts of the past can be transcended and repaired. At this unconscious level the couple will create an unspoken pact, and if these invisible vows are breached the sense of betrayal and confusion is deep.

In exploring how the adult pair bond becomes an attachment relationship, Zeifman and Hazan (2008) draw strong parallels with the journey that the mother and infant take over their first year together. In both cases the common pathway begins with an intense interest in the other, marked by playful flirtatious interactions. As the "falling in love" takes hold, the couple are often found gazing with sustained eye contact; this in turn transitions into an attachment relationship where the mother, or the adult other, serves as an attachment figure. There will be protest on separation and the presence of the other has above all a soothing impact, in contrast to the early days of courtship where the presence of the other was chiefly exciting. The adult couple is distinct from a parent/infant relationship in that the attachment bond is usually reciprocal with both partners able to serve as attachment figure at different times. A key source of couple distress occurs when both partners have a simultaneous need for containment from the other, and we see this most painfully if the couple have a shared attachment wound such as the loss of a child.

We can think of this transition to an attachment relationship as having occurred as soon as the partner becomes the person towards whom attachment behaviour is directed. In a secure couple this means each becomes a source of soothing to the other. When partners have insecure attachment styles, the expression of attachment needs by one would be likely to invoke withdrawing (the avoidant defence) or blaming (an ambivalent strategy). If a couple stay together for *a year or so*, they may transition to a full attachment relationship (Eagle, 2011). Avoidant people often find it harder to make the transition to an attachment bond and are more likely to leave a relationship at this point, perhaps prompted by their unconscious fear of dependency. For young adults with some degree of avoidance, this can be a trigger for coming to therapy – the wish to have conventional family life but a history of always moving on after about eighteen months.

For very insecure people who have found someone traumatised like themselves, this means that the pair transition into an insecure partnership where attachment behaviour is very evident but in its defensive forms of aggression and withdrawal. In these couples, often one partner is strongly avoidant and the other strongly ambivalent. There is no secure base or safe haven, efforts to regulate the self may be interrupted by the other, care-taking may be intrusive as partners regulate *at the expense* of the other, rather than in collaboration. As they begin to self-regulate with their more customary methods there is a risk of laying down a negative cycle in which each is increasingly anxious and alone. These kinds of partnership can suffer domestic violence and if the man is the preoccupied partner and the woman has a dismissing pattern, this may be particularly concerning. When this aggression is male on female, with men commonly having greater strength than women, the danger of physical trauma is especially great. However, it is very important that we recognise the impact of female on male violence as well as that between partners in same sex relationships. The ambivalent partner will be terrified of abandonment and, whether male or female, may protest with aggression if the avoidant partner withdraws.

Sex and avoidance in long-term relationships

Most people have an aspiration to find love and erotic passion within the same relationship. This has been a challenge for human beings in most cultures and avoidant individuals, with their greater capacity to deny their feelings, seem even more prone to separating out the two. Compared to secure and preoccupied people, dismissing individuals are more likely to have one-night stands, to use sex for fun rather than as an expression of emotional depth, and they have less interest in kissing and nuzzling (Feeney, 1999). Addiction of any type can seem like a solution for people who need to keep feelings at bay, and sexual addiction may seem even more inviting now that the internet provides increased accessibility and anonymity.

Avoidant people sometimes hyper-activate the sexual system in order to de-activate the need for attachment and intimacy. In this mindset, a partner might over-emphasise the importance of sexual activity and with this over-expectation of what sex can deliver there can be a hyper-sensitivity and an exaggerated disappointment in a partner's sexual response. An avoidant partner might seek more sex than their partner wants but equally they might find themselves inexplicably turned off sex because their partner's approach is experienced as a demand (and indeed it might well be a disguised entreaty for affection). Where an avoidant and a preoccupied person are coupled there is most risk that they could fall into a pattern of trading sex for affection, with the avoidant person seeking sex and the preoccupied one seeking affection.

Our socialisation around sex still happens along gender roles and this means that gay and lesbian relationships each face a different set of challenges in terms of sexual relating. When both partners are women, there will usually be two people raised to nurture relationships (but not to initiate sex). When both partners are men, there are usually two people socialised to expect the other to nurture relationships (but the self to initiate sex). Onto this base of gender conditioning will be added the different combinations of attachment patterns. In this way of thinking, a couple composed of two men with dismissing patterns would represent the most avoidant possible combination with partners most likely to embark on one-night stands and least likely to stay together for long. Significant age difference may be more common in gay couples and this could also influence the care-giving/ care-seeking dynamic.

Challenges the couple face

In the life cycle of any couple there are bound to be losses: some will be inevitable and some will be cruel blows of fate. Any loss can trigger attachment behaviour and with it our customary defensive patterns; for a dismissing person this means coping through minimisation. Some of the most common losses are: loss of the ideal other; illness and bereavement; becoming parents – or not being able to do so – and infidelity. The first of these is the disillusionment couples face as the idealising projections drop away and they begin to see their partner without a rosy tint. This is the point mentioned above, when avoidant people find it harder to weather that transition from "in love" to an attachment bond.

Illness and bereavement can present a complex challenge for an avoidant partner: the effective and generous instrumental care they offer may be well received, but their lack of empathy and sensitivity may evoke anger and dismay from a distressed partner. When an avoidant person is suffering loss he or she is likely to rebuff support and unlikely to share the pain which is denied to the self. If the loss is a shared one, then at an unconscious level he or she may be using their more preoccupied partner to carry vulnerability for both of them.

The experience of parenting in relation to attachment style was explored by Rholes *et al.* (2006). Their small study of 106 couples is interesting because it looks at the pleasure and satisfaction that parents get from caring for children. Parents with avoidant patterns experienced more stress after the birth and derived less satisfaction from parenting. So the cost was higher and the reward less. Because dismissing people need to maintain deactivation of their attachment systems, they are likely to relate to their children in distant, rejecting ways, just as their parents related to them. If we consider that an avoidant parent would feel less able to seek help with their new challenges, that these individuals have lower overall marital satisfaction and are prone to depression (Mickelson *et al.*, 1997), the picture for an avoidant person becoming a parent is a very challenging one. When a couple are not able to conceive this can be experienced as a serious bereavement but with the complication that the avoidant person may be even less able to acknowledge his or her grief for the longed-for child, and may find it even harder to recognise and process the unconscious experience of failure or exclusion they may be carrying.

Betrayal between partners can be enacted through a wide range of behaviours with sexual infidelity being a common form, and an affair being the most obvious example of this. Because avoidant people tend to feel threatened by the approach of their primary attachment figure, they could be liable to have an affair at the point where a relationship comes to be viewed as permanent. At that point an affair would achieve distance from the partner who is assumed to want more than the avoidant can give. Research indicates that dismissing men and preoccupied women are most likely to have affairs – for an avoidant person an affair can serve to minimise the meaning of the primary relationship (Castellano *et al.*, 2014, p. 76). In contrast, for a preoccupied individual, a liaison may be a way to seek contact and "help" when their long-term relationship is disappointing them. When avoidant people are unfaithful this may be because their relatively low commitment to their romantic partner means they perceive an affair as less of a risk. DeWall *et al.* suggest they "may have less of the commitment-inspired inhibition that normally prevents people from showing interests in alternatives" (2011, p. 1302). Perhaps we can go further and argue that people with high avoidance may achieve a higher sense of security by denying their feelings of commitment. For these individuals feeling dependent on a relationship, that one's wellbeing is tied up with another person, is deeply uncomfortable.

Given that dismissing people are quite prone to having affairs, have less commitment and less pleasure in their relationships, why do they settle in couples at all? Kirkpatrick and Davis (1994) draw on investment theory to explain why people with low satisfaction in a relationship may still stay. In this theory "investment", which signifies time together and shared activities, is weighed against satisfaction; thus, when investment is very high we may stay even if satisfaction is very low. The further factor influencing this choice is the availability of alternatives, and this has been changed recently by the introduction of the internet. If we think in psychodynamic and attachment terms we would understand the "investment" as the ways in which a relationship is providing containment for difficult parts of the self, or perhaps just gives us an arena to re-enact what we have come to expect in relationships.

Divorce

A common presentation in couple therapy is an avoidant/preoccupied pair who arrive for therapy at the point where they are ready to split up. Their therapist tries to tune in to whether the unhappy dynamic between them is protest (with one or both partners actively trying to mend the attachment bond); despair (with hope slipping away); or detachment (where one or both partners have given up). In some cases the preoccupied partner explains that he or she has been pressing their partner to come to therapy for years, but by the time they arrive, the more ambivalent one has often begun to disengage. This preoccupied partner has become what Emotion Focused Couple Therapy calls a worn-out pursuer who has given up the chase. It is because the avoidant one senses that the gap between them has grown wider than is comfortable, even for them, that they can recognise that their preoccupied partner was not crying wolf – there really is a problem needing attention. But by now it may be too late.

Finzi *et al.* (2000) review how attachment style may influence the way divorce impacts on different partners. Even though an avoidant person might leave a relationship more easily than someone with a preoccupied pattern, they can be very hurt to find themselves being divorced, and if they lose composure they may be disturbed by the loss of the façade and of control. If a couple divorce without having children there will be an opportunity for a complete separation which is likely to suit an avoidant person. Where former partners are obliged to collaborate and negotiate about child care, an avoidant partner will be very tested because any contact with a former partner risks triggering attachment feelings and ratcheting up avoidant defences. As they find parenting a challenge under any circumstances, there is a further risk of withdrawal.

Clinical work with avoidant clients

Clinical examples

Sam and Gina came for therapy after years of conflict. Their fights had a clear pattern of Gina making demands and Sam withdrawing. His withdrawal would inflame her need to have her concerns heard, and eventually Sam might be drawn into angry exchanges followed by bouts of silent shame. In terms of the sub-groups discussed above we might understand Sam as being a cool, compliant withdrawer and his wife as a worn-out pursuer. An avoidant partner with a more denigrating defence might be too frightened to engage in therapy at all, and might have insisted that his wife was the one with a problem. Sam, in his False Self desire to do right, was willing to come to sessions and indeed to try to "improve" his behaviour. This attempt to try to get it right almost by rote, may be a function of the group who had an intrusive mother – the children who learnt to down-regulate and to behave in cool, polite, and formal ways. Sam was genuinely puzzled about what his more preoccupied partner wanted; he tried hard to produce the goods, yet I think was consistently resisting intimacy in various passive aggressive ways.

This couple was polarised into a common pursuer/pursued shape. By the time they arrived in my therapy room, any sign of approach by Gina was experienced by Sam as a demand or a reproach; on the other hand, whatever response Sam made tended to be read as disinterest and falling below the standard of care for which Gina was hoping. Sam had agreed to come because he finally realised that Gina might mean her threats about not continuing with the relationship if they did not see a therapist and make changes. The very sad truth, for this couple and for many others, was that by the time Sam realised that his relationship was at risk, Gina had passed a tipping point – her investment in the marriage was ebbing. It was this sense of change in Gina, that she was no longer hammering on his psychic door, that woke Sam up and encouraged him to attend therapy. The concept of the worn-out pursuer succinctly describes this dynamic where one partner has been chronically seeking contact and the other persistently evading intimacy. Eventually the pursuer may lose momentum.

Individuals from any of the avoidant sub groups could fall into this pattern with a partner, but I think that avoidant people with compliant defences are particularly susceptible because they try very hard to please and when they see there really is a problem they agree to come to therapy. Those with a strong defensive devaluing strategy are less able to accept that they have contributed to the difficulty. The compliant group try hard in therapy but are mystified by their partner's demands. Sam had a dutiful False Self and hated to be seen as failing. In couples' therapy he listened carefully to my observations often showing later in a session that he had really taken in a remark, but what he persistently resisted were enquiries about his internal experience. Any amount of empathy or curiosity could be deflected. With some of these couples the prognosis is very sad – they have only arrived in therapy in time for the worn-out pursuer to say goodbye. Sometimes that partner has already found a new relationship and may be bringing the avoidant one to therapy for them to get care, or it may be that the worn-out pursuer had not realised, until therapy made things even clearer, that they had come to the end of their patience.

Mike was not as obviously withdrawing in relationships as Sam and he often used a strategy of care-giving to control distance. His long-term relationship, in which he had been a compulsive carer for his girlfriend, broke down when this girlfriend had an affair. This former partner seems to have taken the needy and sometimes sweet, sometimes naughty child role to Mike's adult and responsible role. While Mike said he was relieved to be free of the burden of being with someone so vulnerable, he almost immediately took in an acquaintance as a lodger – one who seemed to be as needy as his former girlfriend. My sense of this is that Mike tends to seek out partners who will carry his vulnerability and thus help him to feel competent and strong. Likewise, Cheryl was not an obvious withdrawer, her particular avoidant style led her to be always trying to accommodate the other in order to avoid the inconvenience of protest, or of being a disappointment. With her cheery presentation, she was a long way from the common stereotype of a cold, dry Scrooge-like character.

Working with individuals

Whether coming to therapy as individuals or as part of a couple, avoidant people are more likely to judge the therapy negatively. In both cases, in seeking to build a collaborative alliance, we will probably start by meeting the person where they are on the relatively cognitive and judging level; they may need to hear that we respect their doubts and their capacity to appraise the therapy before making a decision about really committing. My work with my client Mike has illustrated much of what we might expect of an avoidant client. His initial motivation for therapy came from his panic attacks and that alarming symptom provided a practical way in to the work; he moved less willingly towards the recognition that he had been depressed throughout much of his life, an experience of bleakness that he had regarded as normal. Often it is somatic episodes that bring an avoidant person to therapy and we need to use this to build some level of alliance swiftly. While preoccupied individuals more often demonstrate depression linked to being swamped with negative thoughts and memories, avoidant people seem to suffer more from depression linked to perfectionism and self-criticism (Zuroff and Fitzpatrick, 1995).

As soon as it is tenable, we aim to challenge avoidant defences through non-complementary responses (Bernier and Dozier, 2002). With Mike, I was initially too accepting of his polite interest in therapy, of his invitation to jointly coast through the sessions. His implicit instruction was: "Don't be interested in this, take it at face value." With deeper reflection on my part, and supervision, my curiosity grew and it became possible to coax Mike into deeper water. Faced with this demand that they "wake up" from their protective "sleep", the avoidant reflex may be anger, dismissal, or withdrawal. Resentful compliance is also a risk and was particularly difficult for Mike and me. Gradually it became more possible to link the flatness in the room to his lifelong pattern of keeping people at bay, and then to recognise how his attachment feelings were being activated in our relationship.

The capacity to explore and to tolerate novelty seems to be lowest in people with avoidant patterns. Mikulincer (1997) found avoidant people to be particularly challenged by the disturbing feelings accompanying curiosity and uncertainty. Having lived with this lack of curiosity and low levels of empathy they are often relatively low in insight; the therapist hopes to engage the avoidant client's interest by describing the shifts and changes in voice, face, and body movements. Clients need us to attune very closely to these shifts, trying to catch what is so ordinary and repeated, and often this is in the body. With Mike it has been his unusual breathing pattern. It took me a while to recognise that I had accepted this as his "normal" and was failing to be curious about a quite distinctive behaviour. Since I woke up to this it has become a gateway to our understanding of his defence.

Therapy puts an avoidant client in a particular bind; Wallin articulates this:

> ...for psychotherapy to provide the secure base that makes such integration [the integration of their dissociated feelings] possible, the therapist has to matter to the patient – and allowing the therapist to matter is, of course, at odds with the deactivating strategy of the dismissing patient, which depends on diminishing the importance of others.
>
> (2007, p. 212)

While some avoidant clients have an overtly denigrating transference others, like Mike, develop an idealising set of projections and these are no less effective as a barrier. Strategies for keeping the therapist at bay can elicit uncomfortable countertransference, though the precise impact will depend on what this transference evokes in the therapist's own internal world. It helps if we can show that the therapy relationship is not like the early parental relationships. Connors describes how staying in the here and now may achieve this: "...focus on the immediate interactive experience in its aliveness and authenticity can facilitate the awakening of the patient's desires and helps the relationship to stay grounded rather than frighteningly coloured by unfounded assumptions" (1997, p. 488).

These are not patients who will benefit from Sphinx-like behaviour. A non-complementary response for an avoidant person requires lively engagement, but in the form of challenge rather than pursuit. Depending on the therapist's own attachment style this may be hard to pull off. Connors sums up possible pitfalls for both the more ambivalent and avoidant therapists: "Clinicians who particularly value being overtly liked and needed by their patients may find avoidant individuals rather frustrating and ungratifying. Therapists who themselves have a more dismissing style might be prone to distance from patients who distance them" (1997, p. 489).

Working with the couple or with "the couple in mind"

When we are thinking about avoidant/ambivalent pairs who are presenting for therapy – whether as a couple or via the preoccupied partner who comes as an individual – there can be tendency to position the avoidant partner as "the problem". Anecdotally we sometimes hear reports suggesting that a female therapist and female client bond over the idea that the client's husband is causing the difficulty because he "doesn't do feelings". This labelling of an absent spouse can blind us to exploring how the two partners between them have created that dynamic. Weeks *et al.* make the point neatly in terms of couple work: "...the therapist must initially walk a tightrope between validating each person's perspective and reframing the problem in such a way that both partners have a role" (2005, p. 14).

I think the same principle applies in individual work: if a new client arrives with a story about a "nightmare partner", we need to validate their experience and support their questioning of the relationship without agreeing that the partner is a bully. Equally, the opposite dynamic can be true: a client might tell of partner's behaviour that we consider abusive and yet they demonstrate an idealising stance towards him or her. In those cases we will not "buy" the idealisation and will probably want to challenge the client about the incongruity they are trying to sustain.

When a person like Sam, with avoidant defences, is "brought" to therapy by a partner, we try to discern whether anger with an unresponsive partner is in the service of mending things, or whether it comes more from the need to punish and allocate blame before leaving. Sometimes there are enough factors keeping the couple together to make this a rich opportunity. In therapy we hope to shake what Tatkin calls the avoidant partner's fantasy of permanence and to wake them up to a "healthy fear of realistic loss" (2009a, p. 14). Once the avoidant partner has been roused from their attachment-passivity and begins to recognise how their unresponsiveness has hurt their spouse, our task is to help contain the huge anxiety they feel in letting go some of their customary defences, as they learn to live with feelings they have avoided for decades. Johnson (2003) describes how the withdrawing partner is often carrying heavy feelings of hopelessness and helplessness that lie behind their avoidant behaviour towards a partner. They may have had doubts from the start about their capacity to provide soothing and reassurance to their "other half", and later, faced with a preoccupied spouse's disappointment, this expectation of failure is proven, like a self-fulfilling prophecy.

In therapy, the aim is often to reduce the dismissing partner's reliance on deactivation and distance and for the couple to increase their capacity to co-regulate. As we work, we track the couple "as a regulatory team" (Tatkin, 2009a, p. 15). We hope for the avoidant partner to become more aware of their habit of under-responding. In a good outcome for a couple, the relationship will become more of a secure base and safe haven: a source of comfort and a place from which they can both go out to explore the world. We would hope for care-seeking and care-giving strategies to be more appropriate and effective, and for the couple to have more confidence in their capacity for repairing ruptures. As in individual therapy, we aim to offer attunement and validation, to promote the experience of feeling understood and contained. We hope to facilitate a connection in which the couple are willing to explore the experience they are having in the room and then to risk new attachment interactions with each other. For clients with dismissing strategies, we would hope for increased capacity to tolerate and share affects and thus to communicate about painful experience without minimising or idealising (they are prone to do this because just thinking about relational needs threatens to destabilise their defence).

Emotion Focused Couple Therapy

In Emotion Focused Couple Therapy (EFCT), Johnson (2012) gives us an important understanding of the cycle of escalation between an avoidant individual and their more preoccupied partner: the more one withdraws the more the other approaches (and vice versa). This is a systemic understanding where the cycle itself is seen as derailing the couple. EFCT aims to de-escalate this cycle and eventually to facilitate positive enactments where partners take risks in sharing more vulnerability than is possible at home.

The initial task, after forming an alliance with the couple, is to get the couple signed up to the concept of the cycle so that they become able to recognise and name it. For an avoidant client this is a significant step; it is an observational and behavioural task and it is achieved above all through validation of the client's experience. The avoidant partner's withdrawing, even abandoning, behaviour is understood in terms of attachment distress, and the repeated reframing of this behaviour is a key aspect of EFCT. Careful listening and enquiry about each partner's experience helps to contain their conflict. If they can come up with their own language to describe their cycle this can become a powerful tool in deepening their understanding. The avoidant partner might experience the other as a train surging towards them, or as a constant pecking, or as a hammering to come in. In turn, a partner might experience them as a barrier, a wall, or a closed door. The therapist then facilitates a deeper recognition of the feelings triggering the repeated behaviours. She might ask the dismissing partner, "When you experience her as 'pecking at you', what's going on inside?". An avoidant individual naturally uses many strategies to avoid going to that internal place from which they could answer this question, and the enquiry may have to be repeated many times in different ways. But the dismissing partner, like anyone else, longs to be understood however much he may also fear it. What we are likely to find is that this withdrawing partner feels helpless, that they have very little belief that they can meet their partner's needs, and that they believe they are bound to be viewed as a disappointment. If this client can allow us to see – and himself to *feel* – his despair, this is a big step. And if a partner is able to respond with empathy, the couple may have an experience of intimacy that has long been missing.

Systemic work

When we work with the couple in the room we have particularly rich material from which to formulate systemic questions. What was he thinking while you were telling me that? What was the look that just passed over her face? What does that mean when he tapers off mid-sentence? These "circular" questions show up patterns rather than facts (Cecchin, 1987). This form of indirect questioning plays to the strengths of how our brains work – we seem to more easily process our thoughts and experience when they are presented as difference. Hence if we ask, "When you lost your house, was that hardest for you or for your wife?" this may be more engaging than the simpler open enquiry, "What was that like, to lose your house?".

With these kinds of observational questions we hope to seed curiosity and confidence in each partner's capacity to understand the other.

We might think of a one-to-one session as a theatre in which attachment strategies are demonstrated; the therapist is standing in for early attachment figures and together client and therapist are enacting some of the key moves from the old script. The staging of the drama may be even more effective in couple therapy because the clients have their actual attachment figure in the room. The therapist has the chance to see first-hand how they relate to this figure, who in some sequences is a stand-in for a parent or sibling. As the content of sessions is focused on the dynamic between the two partners, those with dismissing patterns immediately find themselves in a stressful situation and typically reach for strategies of minimising and withdrawal. This could be low level withdrawal of sitting far apart, looking disinterested, looking away, dismissing what has been said, changing the subject, taking up a position of "I don't understand" without signs of wanting to understand, and not infrequently signalling that they don't find the therapy useful and suggesting that we bring it to an end.

At such a point the therapist has many options. We can attend to the frustration of the avoidant partner, in this case Sam, and perhaps that will enable more connection to the longing that this partner probably has at some level for a more satisfying relationship. Or we can attend to the experience of the more preoccupied partner, Gina, attuning to the feelings that arise from being held at bay and seen as a burden and perhaps that will lead to some deeper recognition of lifelong habits of clinging on to the "other".

Or, the couple therapist can speak of the couple dynamic: "*I think just then was another example of that pattern we have come to know, where you Gina were entreating Sam with an earnest, eager tone of voice, and you Sam, were turned away and adjusting your cuffs. What do we think was going on there?*".

For some couples perhaps a more interpretative comment would be most helpful: *"I think you are showing me how difficult it can feel to manage distance; the pattern you live out each day leaves Gina longing for closeness, to be turned to, and leaves Sam longing for peace, to be left alone."*

Or: *"We know that this is how you each manage yourselves, Gina by seeking comfort through connection and Sam through keeping a private space."*

Or: *"I think just then Gina felt abandoned and Sam felt intruded on, and when you are both very full of your own difficult feelings it is not possible to recognise what is going on for the other."*

Circular questions can also be very fruitful to help explore this dynamic:

- *If an observer were a fly on the wall and perhaps watching this interaction without a sound track, what would they think was going on?*
- *If we were able to track you through the day at home, how many times would we see something like that being repeated?*
- *Who is most troubled by this kind of interaction?*
- *Gina, what does Sam say to himself during this interaction? What does he say to himself afterwards?*
- *Sam, what does Gina say to herself during this interaction? What does she say to herself afterwards?*

For an avoidant partner like Sam, we hope that these enquiries will surprise the unconscious, but not so much as to cause a hardening of defences. Often, circular questions succeed because the person's curiosity is engaged before their defences have detected a threat. Sam protects himself from his internal world, just as he does from Gina, because both of these threaten to flood him with attachment feelings for which he has only this one response of withdrawal–minimisation.

Ultimately, we hope the partners will find more compassion for each other as well as for the self. This may only be achieved if the projective fit can be softened. In this couple, Sam was carrying competence and independence for Gina, who in turn was carrying vulnerability and the longing to attach. To become compassionate towards the other would involve becoming compassionate towards the self. When the projective fit is very strong the couple are unlikely to separate because they "need" that bit which they also despise or fear. In some very painful cases the couple may divorce but remain entangled because the need for that projected part is very real and they are not yet able to carry that within the self.

Conclusion

Intimacy requires "willingness and ability to disclose the true self ... and willingness and ability to rely on one's partner for comfort, support and nurturance" and correspondingly the willingness and ability to provide this for a partner (Collins and Feeney, 2004, p. 173). Both the giving and the receiving are very hard for an avoidant person to do. Rupture and repair is another key pathway by which a relationship is deepened, whether in a therapeutic couple or a romantic couple. Again, these are hard for avoidant people who usually respond to conflict by de-activating the attachment system and withdrawing, being so often governed by their preference for self-reliance rather than collaborative exploration.

Because of their skill in miscuing, these patients can initially mislead us about the degree of their difficulty. With some very avoidant clients I can find it necessary to actively remind myself of the depth of their denied pain. When the distance between the competent False Self and the inner desolation is very great, collapse can be sudden; moreover, ruthlessness and lack of compassion for the self make suicide a risk. Winnicott wrote movingly of these patients who are not initially accessible:

> It is as if a nurse brings a child, and at first the analyst discusses the child's problem, and the child is not directly contacted. Analysis does not start until the nurse has left the child with the analyst, and the child has become able to remain alone with the analyst and has started to play.
>
> (1960, p. 151)

Winnicott then warns us that when the therapist makes contact with the True Self she needs to be ready for a period of extreme dependence. We know from his cases how far he extended himself to be available beyond the expected frame – probably further than we feel able or willing to go. Bowlby also writes of patients with a "highly organised false self" who may need a long period of treatment, but his observations have a more pragmatic tone. This is rather consoling for the therapist who is feeling excluded and defeated by the well-honed strategies of a powerfully avoidant client: "In favourable conditions the ground is worked over first from one angle then from another. At best progress follows a spiral" (Bowlby, 1979, p. 158).

Note

1. All case material has been disguised and assembled from my work with a range of clients.

References

Bartholomew, K. and Horowitz, L. M. (1991). Attachment styles among young adults: A test of a four-category model. *Journal of Personality and Social Psychology*, 61(2), 226.

Bernier, A. and Dozier, M. (2002). The client–counselor match and the corrective emotional experience: Evidence from interpersonal and attachment research. *Psychotherapy: Theory, Research, Practice, Training*, 39(1), 32.

Bowlby, J. (1979). *The Making and Breaking of Affectional Bonds*. London: Tavistock Publications/Routledge.

Castellano, R., Velotti, P., and Zavattini, G. C. (2014). *What Makes Us Stay Together?: Attachment and the Outcomes of Couple Relationships*. London: Karnac.

Cecchin, G. (1987). Hypothesizing, circularity, and neutrality revisited: An invitation to curiosity. *Family Process*, 26(4), 405–413.

Clulow, C. (1998). Gender, attachment and communication in marriage. *Sexual and Marital Therapy*, 13(4), 449–460.

Collins, N. L. and Feeney, B. C. (2004). An attachment theory perspective on closeness and intimacy. In: D. J. Mashek and A. Aron (eds.), *Handbook of Closeness and Intimacy* (pp. 163–187). New Jersey: Lawrence Erlbaum.

Connors, M. E. (1997). The renunciation of love: Dismissive attachment and its treatment. *Psychoanalytic Psychology*, 14(4), 475.

Crittenden, P. M. (1995). Attachment and risk for psychopathology: The early years. *Journal of Developmental & Behavioral Pediatrics*, 16, S12–S16.

Crowell, J. and Treboux, D. (2001). Attachment security in adult partnerships. In: C. Clulow (ed.), *Adult Attachment and Couple Psychotherapy: The "Secure Base" in Practice and Research* (pp. 28–42). Hove, UK: Routledge.

DeWall, C. N., Lambert, N. M., Slotter, E. B., Pond Jr, R. S., Deckman, T., Finkel, E. J., and Fincham, F. D. (2011). So far away from one's partner, yet so close to romantic alternatives: Avoidant attachment, interest in alternatives, and infidelity. *Journal of Personality and Social Psychology*, 101(6), 1302.

Duffell, N. (2000). *The Making of Them: The British Attitude to Children and the Boarding School System*. London: Lone Arrow Press.

Eagle, M. (2011). Attachment and sexuality. In: D. Diamond, S. J. Blatt, and J. D. Lichtenberg (eds.), *Attachment and Sexuality* (pp. 27–50). New York: Routledge.

Feeney, J. A. (1999). Adult romantic attachment and couple relationships. In: J. Cassidy and P. Shaver (eds.), *Handbook of Attachment* (pp. 355–377). New York: Guilford Press.

Feeney, J. A., Noller, P., and Callan, V. J. (1994). Attachment style, communication and satisfaction in the early years. In: K. Bartholomew and D. Perlman (eds.), *Attachment Processes in Adulthood* (pp. 269–308). London: Jessica Kingsley.

Finzi, R., Cohen, O., and Ram, A. (2000). Attachment and divorce. *Journal of Family Psychotherapy*, 11(1), 1–20.

Guerrero, L. K. (1996). Attachment-style differences in intimacy and involvement: A test of the four-category model. *Communications Monographs*, 63(4), 269–292.

Harwood, R. L., Miller, J. G., and Irizarry, N. L. (1995). *Culture and Attachment: Perceptions of the Child in Context*. New York: Guilford Press.

Holmes, J. (2001) Foreword. In: C. Clulow (ed.), *Adult Attachment and Couple Psychotherapy: The "Secure Base" in Practice and Research* (pp. XIII–XX). Hove, UK: Routledge.

Johnson, S. M. (2003). Attachment theory: A guide for couple therapy. In: S. M. Johnson and V. E. Whiffen (eds.), *Attachment Processes in Couple and Family Therapy* (pp. 103–123). New York: Guilford Press.

Johnson, S. M. (2012). *The Practice of Emotionally Focused Couple Therapy: Creating Connection*. Hove, UK: Routledge.

Jung, C. G. (2014). The development of personality. (R. F. C. Hull, trans.). In: H. Read, M. Fordham, G. Adler, and W. McGuire (series eds.), *The collected works of C. G. Jung* (Vol. 17). London: Routledge. (Original work published 1958).

Kirkpatrick, L. A., and Davis, K. E. (1994). Attachment style, gender, and relationship stability: A longitudinal analysis. *Journal of Personality and Social Psychology*, 66(3), 502.

Mickelson, K. D., Kessler, R. C., and Shaver, P. R. (1997). Adult attachment in a nationally representative sample. *Journal of Personality and Social Psychology*, 73(5), 1092.

Mikulincer, M. (1995). Attachment style and the mental representation of the self. *Journal of Personality and Social Psychology*, 69(6), 1203.

Mikulincer, M. (1997). Adult attachment style and information processing: Individual differences in curiosity and cognitive closure. *Journal of Personality and Social Psychology*, 72(5), 1217–1230.

Power, A. (2013). Early boarding: Rich children in care, their adaptation to loss of attachment. *Attachment: New Directions in Relational Psychoanalysis and Psychotherapy*, 7(2), 186–201.

Power, A. (2018). What kind of courtship sets a couple up for long term attachment: Romance, arranged marriage or online match-making? *Attachment: New Directions in Relational Psychoanalysis and Psychotherapy* (in press).

Reibstein, J. (1998). Attachment, pain and detachment for the adults in divorce. *Sexual and Marital Therapy*, *13*(4), 351–360.

Rholes, W. S., Simpson, J. A., and Friedman, M. (2006). Avoidant attachment and the experience of parenting. *Personality and Social Psychology Bulletin*, *32*(3), 275–285.

Schaverien, J. (2015). *Boarding School Syndrome: The Psychological Trauma of the "Privileged" Child*. Hove, UK: Routledge.

Simpson, J. A., Winterheld, H. A., Rholes, W. S., and Oriña, M. M. (2007). Working models of attachment and reactions to different forms of caregiving from romantic partners. *Journal of Personality and Social Psychology*, *93*(3), 466.

Solomon, M. and Tatkin, S. (2011). *Love and War in Intimate Relationships: Connection, Disconnection, and Mutual Regulation in Couple Therapy*. New York: W. W. Norton.

Tatkin, S. (2009a). I want you in the house, just not in my room … unless I ask you: The plight of the avoidantly attached partner in couples' therapy. *New Therapist Magazine*, *62*, 10–16.

Tatkin, S. (2009b). Addiction to "alone time": Avoidant attachment, narcissism, and a one-person psychology within a two-person psychological system. *The Therapist*, *57*, 37–45.

Tidwell, M. C. O., Reis, H. T., and Shaver, P. R. (1996). Attachment, attractiveness, and social interaction: A diary study. *Journal of Personality and Social Psychology*, *71*(4), 729.

van IJzendoorn, M. H. and Kroonenberg, P. M. (1988). Cross-cultural patterns of attachment: A meta-analysis of the strange situation. *Child Development*, *59*, 147–156.

Wallin, D. J. (2007). *Attachment in Psychotherapy*. New York: Guilford Press.

Weeks, G., Odell, M., and Methven, S. (2005). *If Only I Had Known … : Avoiding Common Mistakes in Couples Therapy*. New York: Norton.

Winnicott, D. W. (1960). Ego distortion in terms of true and false self. In: D. W. Winnicott (1965), *The Maturational Processes and the Facilitating Environment* (pp. 140–152). London: Hogarth Press.

Zeifman, D. and Hazan, C. (2008). Pair bonds as attachments: Re-evaluating the evidence. In: J. Cassidy and P. R. Shaver (eds.), *Handbook of Attachment: Theory, Research, and Clinical Applications*. 2nd edn. (pp. 436–455). New York: Guilford Press.

Zuroff, D. C. and Fitzpatrick, D. K. (1995). Depressive personality styles: Implications for adult attachment. *Personality and Individual Differences*, *18*(2), 253–265.

CHAPTER FOUR

Masters in the art of defence: shame and defences against intimacy

Linda Cundy

Introduction

Defences mark the spot where pain is buried, a flag in the ground indicating the presence of a deeply buried narcissistic wound. This chapter outlines the core anxieties of avoidant individuals and highlights the myriad of creative strategies used to keep others at a safe emotional distance. In so doing, their internal worlds and their relationships with themselves are explored. It then addresses psychotherapy with avoidant clients, how we can find empathy for people who may be dismissing of our efforts and difficult to make a relationship with. Finally, it focuses on the therapeutic aims when working with this group of patients, helping them become less defended and inhibited, more spontaneous and alive in relationships.

The clinical examples I give are compounds constructed in each case from two or more specific individuals. For the sake of clarity, I refer to clients in general using the masculine pronoun, and to the therapist using the feminine. This is not intended to suggest that dismissing attachment is more prevalent in men, and that has not been my experience in the consulting room.

Adaptation

Attachment theory is an evolutionary model positing that the instinct to form strong bonds with parent figures has ensured survival for each of us. Herbert Spencer (1864) wrote about "the survival of the fittest", the evolutionary advantage of being adapted to the environment we inhabit. As human beings, we have shaped our geographical environment, but each baby is born into a unique relational microclimate influenced by culture, religion, economic realities, historical factors, and parental "aesthetics" (Bollas, 1987). How each parent relates to other people, to him- or herself, and how they are in the world is in turn an expression of their own attachment history.

Babies are born "unfinished", with a remarkable capacity to adapt and fit into their family and social context. However, their environment also needs to adjust to accommodate the new arrival, and difficulties can arise if the infant is expected to do all the work to fit into a niche created by parental needs and fantasies. We may think, for instance, of situations where there are already numerous children, where mother is depressed or narcissistic or ill, or where father has firm ideas about what is required of this new child. In such circumstances, the infant is obliged to become the child his parents wish him to be, regardless of his own needs and proclivities. Winnicott refers to this as the development of a "False Self" (1960), where the child's creativity is stymied in favour of the parental vision. The infant learns to inhibit his own innate liveliness or override his own quiet way of being in order to find a place for himself within his particular family system.

> Instead of having felt recognized and accepted as himself, his own potential being nurtured, the child has become inhabited by his mother's fantasy. Whilst to some extent all human identities are false, insofar as we have to construct a "self" on the basis of the roles and images available in the pre-existing culture into which we are born, this process becomes more tilted in the direction of pathology when the mother's narcissism takes precedence over her concern to recognize and nurture her particular child. The more authentic self then becomes an embarrassment and a source of anxiety.
>
> (Mollon, 2002, p. 17)

Defences are accommodations, where the self is edited in order to fit in. They protect us from impinging over-stimulation, and from the pain of narcissistic wounds, from awareness that we are not quite the child that our caregivers wanted, and the resultant shame. We can see these defensive processes in operation in very young infants in the form of gaze aversion (Main and Weston, 1982; Tronick, 2007; Tronick et al., 1978) or turning the head away from intrusive attention. By twelve to fifteen months in the Strange Situation Test, we see some toddlers not only failing to make eye contact or to seek proximity with the parent but also inhibiting any signs of the anxiety or distress we would expect in a child put under the strain of brief separation in an unfamiliar environment. "The 'avoidant' infant, who attends to the parent's comings or goings but conceals its distress in favour of maintaining a distal minimized relationship, treads a thin line between the loneliness of abandonment and the pain of rebuff" (Holmes, 1996, p. 55). Before they have language they are already containing themselves, hiding their true feelings from attachment figures. And before much longer, many are hiding their emotions from themselves.

In order to deny the impact of narcissistic wounding, memories and the emotions attached to them must be repressed. Bowlby pointed out that "observation of the onset of detached behaviour in a child who is spending a few weeks in strange surroundings away from his mother is as close as we can get to observing repression actually occurring" (1969/1991, p. 6). This is clearly evident in the film of 17-month-old John, who spent nine days in a residential nursery while his mother gave birth to her second child (Robertson and Robertson, 1969). It is painful to watch this small child struggling to contain his distress, and we witness the moments he shuts down his previously spontaneous feelings. The outcome of this repression is clearly visible when his mother arrives to collect him.

Alice Miller (1980/1987) wrote about the impact of particular child-rearing practices in moulding children into acquiescent, unquestioning, well-behaved citizens. She cites the advice of numerous "poisonous pedagogues" who viewed children as manipulative and wilful. Corporal punishment was advocated, as was withholding affection or attention, and deliberately humiliating children to "break their spirits" – all in the name of kindness. Thus, cruelty was justified as benefitting the child, calling to mind the Biblical aphorism, "He who withholds his rod hates his son" (Proverbs 13: 24).

Harsh physical chastisement is no longer considered acceptable in much of the world (though as I write this, there is wide debate about banning parents from smacking children in England and Wales, with many voices raised in opposition to the proposed new law) but there are other, more subtle, approaches to ensure that children will be undemanding, self-contained, disciplined, and undemonstrative that are culturally sanctioned. In the 1950s and 1960s, the child-rearing system of Frederic Truby King became common practice, with an emphasis on routine and discipline: four-hourly feeds, the baby left to cry between feeds rather than being held and soothed, and with plenty of fresh air. Such techniques (reinvented in the noughties by Gina Ford) ensure that infants quickly learn what is required of them: to be seen (sometimes) but not heard; to despair of getting their needs for comfort, reassurance, interaction, and delight met. These needs are perceived as manipulative, unacceptable, and shameful, rather than viewed as simply inconvenient to parents.

Babies are acutely sensitive to the approval and disapproval of their parents and "curate" themselves accordingly – "to curate" is to "select, organize and present" (https://en.oxforddictionaries.com). Attachment researchers have found that disapproval and rejection of the infant's needs for comfort feature in avoidant relationships between mothers and young children in both the home and laboratory settings. According to Main and Weston, "avoidance is highly associated with the mother's anger, her emotional inexpressiveness, and her rejection of physical contact with the infant" (1982, p. 32). They cite examples from their Strange Situation research in Baltimore: "Mothers of mother-avoidant infants mocked their infants or spoke sarcastically to or about them; some stared them down. One expressed irritation when the infant spilled imaginary tea" (ibid., p. 46).

These mothers do not appear to inhibit their critical behaviour despite being observed. Their lack of attunement or empathy for their little ones does not feel shameful to them, but perhaps the infants themselves feel shame at not being lovable to the person they love most – and in time they will not feel acceptable to themselves. They become averse to intimate contact with others, partly due to feeling unworthy, inadequate, and contemptible, but also, perhaps, for fear of their own longing for love and acceptance being unleashed.

The degree of avoidance

"Avoidance" refers to the tendency to evade intimacy with other people, but also to defend against certain feelings, impulses, memories, and needs that arise internally. Not surprisingly, this exists on a spectrum according to what was required in the early environment, from mild or situational to extreme, from adaptive to pathological. For instance, some families are unable to tolerate a clingy or angry baby but are accepting of a happy, playful baby, while others are unable to bear any sign of the child's liveliness. In some situations, the child is criticised, while in others he is hit, ignored, or basically abandoned. "Avoidant attachment should be seen as a predisposition to pathology rather than as a disorder in itself – a rigidity that may mean that when circumstances change difficulties come to the surface" (Holmes, 1996, p. 23). Defences may only become obvious when an individual is under duress (such as conflict with a spouse, a relationship ending, bereavement, and so on), or may be pervasive, dominating the personality. In northern European cultures, some of these traits may be considered desirable – we would not expect our surgeons, business leaders, or diplomats to be emotionally volatile, and in northern Europe we tend to disapprove of our politicians when their intense feelings are acted out rather than contained.

The traits of dismissing attachment, including self-control, a strong work ethic, high standards, and self-reliance can be useful in many spheres and are found in psychotherapists but also in psychopaths! In some cases, defences developed when the child's need to give and receive love was rejected, causing a narcissistic wound. The child may have edited his emotions and reined in his playfulness to fit in with parental requirements. But some children learn early on to defend themselves against dysregulating intrusions caused, for instance, by mother's anxiety or anger; and for yet others there would have been a history of gross trauma and neglect requiring the child to cut off feelings and trust, becoming self-sufficient in order to survive in a hostile microclimate.

Avoidant states of mind

The capacity to adapt to variations in our environment is present throughout life, and we pick up fairly subtle changes, such as the transient shift in atmosphere created by the moods of other people, or the impact of being around someone with a secure, preoccupied, dismissing, or disorganised pattern of attachment. We modify ourselves accordingly. This is a particularly valuable skill for psychotherapists, as we can feel the pull to adapt ourselves to each client and think about what that may be communicating. Highly defended children and adults are likely to feel differently around others who are likewise restrained compared to the experience of being with someone who demands interaction, intimacy, and a sharing of minds. And we hope that as therapists we are secure enough to allow avoidant clients to gradually drop their defences and become more expansive, less inhibited, more relational.

So should we think of "avoidant states of mind" rather than static attachment categories? Perhaps, but I believe that there are certain core patterns, a kind of default setting that we return to when we feel under duress. In these moments we resort to what is familiar, the way of being that has kept us safe, and this is usually the pattern of attachment that evolved within our first environment. I give examples here of three clients who grew up in totally different situations but who have in common a core pattern of attachment that we recognise as dismissing.

Case examples

Wes

Wes suffered appalling neglect from the start due to his mother's addiction to Class A drugs and her resultant chaotic lifestyle that also involved prostitution. She often forgot about him and he remembers being locked in a room alone for many hours, cold, dirty, and hungry. He was an invisible child. When one of his mother's boyfriends moved in, nothing improved. He witnessed the man, also an addict, attacking his mother, and she began to protect herself by accusing the child of naughtiness, inciting her partner to beat him instead.

Wes felt impotent and humiliated but tried to contain his rage. His adolescence was marked by acts of petty crime but he joined the armed forces at the earliest opportunity as this offered him a way out of his grim environment. He wanted something better for himself, and the military option provided structure, discipline, purpose, and containment. It also gave him a focus for the murderous rage he carried. But once he was demobilised he began to drift and his drinking got out of control. He became involved with a very vulnerable woman who let him move into her home, but she complained that he spent too much time with his friends, other veterans, and told him to leave. In a rage, Wes lashed out at her. He was convicted of assault and committing actual bodily harm and served a prison sentence for the offence.

When I met him, Wes had been sober for over a decade and was using twelve-step groups for support, but he was very isolated. He struggled to make relationships and had difficulty empathising with people – he seemed cut off from all feelings. The only contact he had with others outside his Alcoholics Anonymous meetings was conducted online; he had trained in information technology and was able to work from home troubleshooting computer problems.

Very early in life, the message for Wes was that he could not rely on anybody. He developed coping strategies that helped him survive but he could not make meaningful relationships. His rage was dissociated but could be triggered if he felt humiliated and it was then uncontrollable. He felt contempt for women, but also for himself as a child. His relational history created the conditions for a core pattern of attachment that mixed dismissing defences with unresolved complex trauma. It was surprising that he found his way to therapy.

Oliver

In contrast, Oliver was born to middle class parents who were wrapped up in their careers and with each other. They worked together from home running a business that was the major focus of their lives. It seems that Oliver's birth was traumatic, following a difficult pregnancy. At our first meeting I asked why he thought he was an only child. He replied: "My father told me that he nearly lost my mother when I was born."

Oliver was materially comfortable but an overlooked child, a good boy who caused his parents no trouble. They did not notice his unhappiness or anxiety. He learned to inhibit his liveliness, to be quiet and constrained. He remembers an occasion when, playing pirates, he ran into the kitchen, accidentally knocking into his mother who scalded herself with boiling water. That memory still causes him shame.

As a lonely boy he lived a great deal in his imagination. Unlike Wes, Oliver did not avoid his internal world but guarded it fiercely as his own private realm. He populated it with imaginary people who cared about him and loved him unconditionally. He became loyal to these figments of his imagination, these perfectly attuned characters who had no needs of their own to intrude or compete for attention. But real people were another matter, and he did not accept that he could ever be desirable.

As an adult, Oliver has a circle of friends who perceive him as a great raconteur, intelligent, funny, and confident. But his self-confidence is all show. He has a highly critical and punitive superego, a cruel internal saboteur (Fairbairn, 1952/1994) that is hell-bent on spoiling any pleasure in life, preventing him from enjoying the love of his friends or any sense of achievement in his work. He does not feel deserving of admiration. He is extremely critical of himself but much more forgiving of other people's failings. He cannot allow anyone to get close enough to see the person he feels himself to be – a worthless man. There is an air of depression about him that I suspect has haunted him all his life, the result of so much inhibition. He never felt he was important to his parents, especially his mother, and there is shame about this. At a recent session he told me: "Somewhere deep in my being I believe I have done something wrong." I replied, "I think you feel that you *are* something wrong." He cried.

Ayesha

Ayesha told me that her childhood had been "fine, normal, a bit privileged I suppose". She grew up in an immaculate home, kept spotless by her mother whose obsessive–compulsive disorder dominated the family and who demanded cleanliness, order, and self-control of the children. Her husband, Ayesha's father, had high expectations of them in other ways. From an immigrant background, he had worked his way up through his profession to financial security and status, but he demanded that his children achieved more, to bring respectability to the family. He wanted to put distance between himself and his past; there seems to have been some unspoken trauma in his history. The children were primed to excel at school and university, to make stellar careers, and mix with movers and shakers.

Ayesha suffered from a skin condition that was repugnant to her mother. Physical appearance and hygiene were major preoccupations at home, and Ayesha was banned from entering the kitchen when her rashes flared up. She experienced her mother's anxiety as suffocating and intrusive, and she came to hate her own body. Puberty was particularly difficult as she felt out of control. She noticed the alarm on her mother's face as her adolescent body grew and her periods began. She longed to be invisible.

Ayesha adopted a "no-entry defence" (Williams, 1997/2002) to protect herself from her mother's intrusive anxiety, criticism, and fussing. She recalls: "I decided that I would never ask for anything because of what would be unleashed if I made myself visible."

Meanwhile she studied over and above what was expected of her, often missing sleep and meals in order to revise or put extra effort into her homework. She asked to go to boarding school to devote more energy to her studies, hoping to win a place at Oxbridge. It was here, at boarding school, that anorexia began to get a grip on her. During school holidays, her father did not notice how very thin she had become, but her mother praised her for "managing to diet".

She earned her place at an Oxford college, gained a first class degree and an offer of a good job with prospects for an impressive career, but the eating disorder was by now a serious threat to her life. She was admitted as an inpatient at a specialist unit where she received psychotherapy. As she was preparing to be discharged she contacted me to set up private therapy to support her recovery. When I met her she was immaculately dressed in designer labels and it was hard to read her facial expressions through a mask of perfectly applied make-up.

Ayesha had a boyfriend in America and their relationship was conducted mostly online and through text messages. When they did meet up she felt smothered by him. She was contemptuous of herself for what she perceived to be her weakness, but also felt contempt for him when he was upset by her rejections. She had a tendency to mock anybody, including myself, who she perceived to be needy, "hysterical", "banging on about feelings", irrational, or intellectually inferior. But as time passed I began to see another side to her.

She is ambitious and driven in her work but haunted by an expectation of failure. She detests being perceived as intelligent, believing that she is a fraud who is only skilled at deception. Her defences are brittle and fragile. Her therapy has taken many years to develop, and for much of that time it was impossible for her to acknowledge any attachment to me, although she could occasionally admit to valuing the structure provided by weekly sessions. For a long time I felt I was earning the trust of a wild animal that could at any moment be spooked and either attack or bolt.

These three individuals are very different but have something in common. Each needed to adapt – or try to adapt – to fit a relational environment that did not adjust to accommodate their ordinary needs or their unique qualities in infancy. In order to edit the self to suit parental requirements, each developed a range of defences to contain themselves, to dissociate from their feelings, to regulate the distress of narcissistic wounds and the shame arising from believing themselves to be fundamentally defective. The core anxiety is that of being seen, exposed, intruded upon, judged, criticised, humiliated, colonised, and shamed.

According to Mitchell and Black:

> Gradually, incrementally but inevitably, the self-system shapes the child to fit into the niche supplied by the personalities of his significant others. The myriad potentialities of the child become slowly and inexorably honed down as he becomes the son of this particular mother, of this particular father. The outline of the child's personality is sharply etched by the acid of the parents' anxiety.
>
> (1995, pp. 69–70)

Through attachment-based psychotherapy we aim to create a new relational environment, to mobilise clients' continuing capacity to adapt. In so doing, we need to help them in the process of dismantling defences against being close with others, challenge their critical internal voices, and provide the model for a new internal object that will soothe, encourage, delight in, and celebrate their achievements. They must also be helped to let go of shame. I return to these therapeutic tasks later.

Defences

Avoidant individuals are masters in the art of evasion and disguise, employing a remarkable range of defensive manoeuvres that indicate the quality of their relationships with other people. These are also suggestive of the *feel* of the individual's internal world, and the dynamics at play in his relationship with himself. Defensive strategies are utilised against intrusions from the outside world, but also against feelings, memories and fantasies arising in the internal world. Layers of resistance against making connections between "domains" (inner world and external reality; past, present, and future; dreams and waking life; relationship with the therapist and relationships outside the consulting room, etc.) can make therapy feel dull, lifeless; without these links the narrative is bland and two-dimensional.

Self-protective measures can include inflated grandiosity, contempt for others, bullying, arrogance, and anger used as a smokescreen to hide behind. "Workaholism" – a strong work ethic, need for targets and deadlines, and a driven sense of ambition, are often found. The by-products of this way of being are professional identity, respect, status, and a kind of "security" that comes from financial rewards. Work also provides an ideal excuse for avoiding unwanted family and social occasions. Avoidant individuals seem more comfortable focusing on the future, rather than the past. They usually prefer action, working towards a goal, rather than relaxing in the company of other people, or sitting alone with their memories.

Self-control, controlling the degree of intimacy in relationships, and controlling one's environment have complex defensive functions. Extreme cleanliness, exercise, and dietary restriction can be seen as an attempt to tame one's appetites rather than allow any messy needs to be acknowledged or seen by other people. Also, with so much effort directed toward these struggles, there is little mental space to attend to uncomfortable emotions or memories.

I worked with a woman whose obsessive–compulsive disorder was manifested in housework. She had constructed detailed routines for cleaning that had to be followed to the letter in a specific order, without missing any of the steps. She would be unable to leave home until the routine had been completed in sequence from start to finish. This included disinfecting light switches every day and washing the underside of tables and chairs. In therapy, she spoke of growing up in a household with parents who frequently argued and fought. She learned to numb her distress by obsessively polishing the wooden floor in the hallway, and this also earned her some approval when her mother noticed. Housework continued to provide effective, ritualistic protection against her anxiety and anger, helping her block upsetting memories – as long as she submitted to the tyranny of her self-imposed "rules".

For this woman, the imperative was to avoid her internal world with its memories of cruelty and hardship, and her ritualistic activity provided an effective firewall to screen these out. For some, though, it is the anxiety of current relationships that must be managed, and self-medication of various kinds may be resorted to in order to disguise or hide their discomfort in public. Smoking, drinking, and the use of certain kinds of substances may be used to bolster confidence or, as with Oliver, a false persona may be adopted to present a version of the self that is charming, witty, apparently at ease, and with a self-deprecating sense of humour. Social anxiety can be excruciating for people who anticipate ridicule, coldness, or rejection. They fear making fools of themselves, exposing too much of what they believe to be their defective selves.

Denial is an effective shield against narcissistic pain. In the Adult Attachment Interview (AAI), interviewees classified as having a dismissing pattern of attachment tend to downplay the significance of events that would be expected to cause distress. And in the consulting room we may often hear a client minimising the impact of an unloving childhood: *"It didn't hurt"*; *"It didn't affect me"*; *"They didn't mean it"*; *"That's how it was in those days"*; *"It did me good"*. The client would prefer not to reflect on such things but when asked directly he rationalises the harsh treatment meted out to a child – himself. It is possible that he has never given any thought to why his attachment figures behaved as they did, or he may defend them through a precocious understanding of the difficulties they were coping with: *"My father was not a cruel man but he grew up in a children's home and didn't know how to be a parent"* or *"I know my mother loved me although she didn't show it. It was hard for her because I was always in trouble at school."*

This apparent ability to see the bigger picture is misleading: the person's understanding and "forgiveness" for his caregivers is at the expense of real compassion for himself as a child. He shoulders the burden of responsibility for his own unhappiness. This is in keeping with Fairbairn's notion of the moral defence, also termed "the defence of the super-ego" (1952/1994). It is easier for a child to believe himself unworthy of love than to perceive his "objects" – his attachment figures – as incapable of loving him.

> The essential feature, and indeed the central aim, of this defence is the conversion of an original situation in which the child is surrounded by bad objects into a new situation in which his objects are good and he himself is bad.
>
> (1952/1994, p. 68)

In keeping with attachment theory, Fairbairn recognises that the child must protect his parents because he needs them, but his survival strategy comes at a high price, including the lifelong relationship with a critical superego and the pervasive sense of guilt and shame that Fairbairn alludes to.

Along with denial, as we have seen, goes self-denial. Anna Freud (1936/1993) described certain phenomena that she equated with adolescence; the development of asceticism and intellectualisation that "serve to defend the individual from the instinctual demands of the body" (1936/1993, p. 152). Of course, these attitudes also protect against instinctual needs for relating and intimacy. They are commonly found in the avoidant person's armoury: emotions are denigrated, rational thought is reified, and self-discipline is essential if shaming exposure is to be avoided. The discipline required to resist eating, to work long hours without sleep, or to deny oneself pleasure while pursuing exceptional achievement are an extension of inflexible self-containment – rigidly holding oneself together and keeping the outside world at bay.

Thinking of the repudiation of normal intimacy needs, I am reminded of "Anna", the interviewee described by Oskis (Chapter 2), whose Attachment Style Interview (ASI) indicated "an avoidant style characterised by high self-reliance and high constraints on closeness, and there is neither fear of rejection, nor high anger" (p. 28). I suggest that Anna's longing for closeness, her anxiety regarding rejection, and her anger were all subject to self-denial, kept hidden away and actively avoided, rather than not being present at all.

Asceticism may in part be employed as a punishment for perceived flaws and failures. While some avoidant individuals amass material goods and wealth in place of internal security, others may have developed a certain kind of morality to justify depriving themselves of comfort: *"It's disgusting to eat so much when there are people starving in the world"*; *"I may be ill but others have it worse so I have to keep going"*; *"I feel bad about being so privileged – I am a waste of the world's resources."* There develops a sadomasochistic relationship with the self as the avoidant person punishes himself and denies himself comfort. Not only is there the presence of a punitive, demanding internal object, there is an absence of another kind of internal resource – a more kindly, accepting, soothing presence. I will return to this later.

Self-hatred may be disguised through self-deprecating humour aimed at entertaining and distracting others. It is a form of hiding in plain sight, a double bluff, drawing peoples' attention and amusing them with anecdotes that present oneself as foolish, ignorant, clumsy, arrogant, fat, or ugly. The audience is primed to believe that the entertainer is robust and tolerant of his own flaws, comfortable with exposing these quirks because he is, fundamentally, accepting of himself. They may not notice the depth of attack and self-loathing hidden behind the witty throwaway remarks.

Further strategies used to hide in plain sight and manipulate others concern appearance. Again, there are a number of opportunities for creativity in this defence. On the one hand, it is possible to keep others at arm's length by presenting oneself as aggressive, with clothing, hairstyle, tattoos, and piercings aimed at intimidation. A certain provocative or threatening attitude completes the picture, with the message, "*I'm not good news, not someone you want to mess with*" or perhaps, "*Accept me as I am or f*** off – I don't need you.*" The real meaning of this visual statement is: "*See this disguise, don't see <u>me</u>.*" Expecting rejection, these individuals provoke it. This gives some sense of control and distracts from the pain of feeling unacceptable – it is better to be angry than wounded.

A variant of this distancing tactic is perfect, flawless presentation, the immaculately groomed, exquisitely beautiful, untouchable creature that may be worshipped from afar but never approached. The effort put into this illusion of perfection indicates its true purpose – to prevent the real self from being scrutinised and judged.

Defences against intrusion

The vision of loveliness and the seemingly threatening provocative character are guisards – people in disguise. They have developed strategies to protect the self from being "rumbled", viewed critically, and found wanting. High standards, judgement, and fault-finding may well have characterised their relationships in infancy and childhood. Being on the receiving end of a disapproving glare from those who are most loved is an experience of shame that gets inside us as an impingement, forming the core of an "unempathic internal object" (Mollon, 1993, p. 60).

Impingement of a different kind can happen when attachment figures are misattuned and intrusive. Rather than reading the infant's communications and responding to his mood, these caregivers force themselves, their personalities, and needs onto him. This may be in the form of loud voices and overly energetic handling, or of poking the child to keep him awake or make him "perform". I worked with a woman whose father was on the autistic spectrum. His inability to attune to her in later life made us wonder about how he had been when she was tiny, and we concluded that she might have learned to turn away from his dysregulating presence in order to preserve herself. In adult life she preferred to live alone with only her dog and books for company.

Where a child experiences his parents projecting their anxiety or anger into him – if, for instance, he is shouted at or force fed – he will need to preserve his psychic integrity by shutting down relating. Closing eyes, turning the head away, and averting gaze are all attempts used by even small babies to occlude the source of distress. Later, they may discover more sophisticated strategies to distract themselves, including the "no entry defence" referred to above in the vignette of Ayesha. Gianna Williams highlights the role of this system of defences and the underlying anxieties thus:

> A pervasive symptomatology with a 'no-entry' quality can represent a defensive system developed by a child who has perceived himself/herself (early in infancy), to have been invaded by projections. These projections are likely to have been experienced by him or her as persecutory foreign bodies. The 'no-entry' syndrome performs the defensive function of blocking access to any input experienced as potentially intrusive and persecutory.
>
> (1997/2002, p. 121)

We see here the more complex defensive manoeuvres that become available beyond infancy as cognitive capacities mature: the baby's self preserving instinct to close his eyes or turn his head away is perhaps a precursor to denial, a psychological refusal to see. Ascetic self-denial and intellectualisation are further levels of defence that develop later.

Social relationships

Ayesha and Oliver have large friendship groups; in fact, I would describe them both as loyal, thoughtful friends. But neither of them really revealed themselves in their social circles. Friendship groups can provide companionship without the intimacy of one-to-one relating. Parties and get-togethers do not require deep sharing of self, exchanging confidences, exposing raw feelings, or asking for help.

Human beings are social animals and most people, even those with a history of trauma, still want to relate to others. Belonging to a community or social group may provide opportunities for important aspects of relating, including occasions to show care to others. Being part of a community, being known to others and accepted as belonging, contributes to a sense of identity, whether it is a church congregation, supporters of a football team, members of a voluntary organisation, or an online social network.

For some, shyness and social awkwardness make everyday encounters a painful challenge. A different form of companionship, for instance with animals or even inanimate objects, is preferable.

Relating with and through technology

Certain kinds of romantic relationship suit dismissing people, who need to carefully regulate the emotional space between themselves and other people. Long-distance relationships, affairs with someone who is practically or emotionally unavailable, or online virtual relationships may be appealing, if not ultimately satisfying. The illusion of intimacy may be created in virtual worlds, where avatars can meet, fall in love, and make a life together. But this is not real life with the ordinariness of everyday routines and the potential for both conflict and genuine intimacy.

Technology can provide a means of connecting with others, but also functions as a screen between self and other, or a filter so relationships and intimacy can be controlled. It is possible that digital technologies are creating a more avoidant society (Cundy, 2015; Greenfield, 2008, 2015; Turkle, 2005, 2011, among others). When Alexander Graham Bell invented the telephone, it became possible to speak to loved ones who were not physically present. From public telephone boxes to the landline phone at home, and then the mobile, we were able to converse in real time and maintain connection across geographical space and time zones. But with the advent of smartphones and various apps, our communication has shifted from the spoken word to text, from email to emoji, from rich emotionally informed language to Twitter and Instagram. These new modes of communication no doubt suit avoidant individuals who prefer relationship without intrusion, who want connectivity but without emotional connection, or who choose "life in two dimensions" (Greenfield, 2008). As the possibilities provided by the internet and computer technology make remote working more common, so the challenges of workplace life alongside colleagues can also be avoided. Meanwhile globalisation means that more careers involve working away from home from time to time, with implications for relationships with partners and children.

For some avoidant individuals, digital devices are more than a means to connect – they come to replace human beings as companions. Devices are more or less reliable and predictable. In public spaces, being engaged with a screen creates the illusion of existing in a bubble, preventing the approach or intrusion of other people. Technology provides a kind of psychic retreat (Steiner, 1993).

A patient recently noted ruefully: "We are humanising robots and dehumanising people." We have become accustomed to the satnav and, more recently, to Siri and Alexa – voice-activated "personal assistants" that turn on your lighting and heating, play the music you request, perform internet searches, make lists dictated to them, and answer simple questions with a bright, cheery, female voice. We are not so far away from the scenario of *Her*, a film by Spike Jonze (2014) about a man falling in love with a responsive personalised operating system voiced by Scarlett Johansson. The illusion of a virtual other who is attentive, reliable, helpful, non-judgemental, unthreatening, and undemanding must be a great temptation to someone who finds real human company uncomfortable but who has not become entirely detached from the instinct to relate: "I find people willing to seriously consider robots not only as pets but as potential friends, confidants, and even romantic partners" (Turkle, 2011, p. 9). I imagine most of those Turkle refers to would fit the dismissing attachment category.

Secondary defences

Not all babies discover the "avoidant defences" early on. If there is just a little inconsistency in the parents' responses to his attachment communications, this keeps open the possibility of persuading them to pay closer attention, to be more sensitive to his needs. In other words, the child has not yet given up hope. He may protest vigorously at separation or loss of connection. If this is occasionally successful, he may become completely focused on the relationship and an ambivalent pattern of attachment evolves between himself and his caregiver. However, if his protestation and demands meet consistently with coldness, hostility, rejection, or abandonment, he may eventually despair of ever getting a helpful response.

Abandoning the attachment-eliciting strategies of crying, screaming, or clinging, he comes to accept his lot, to be quiet and uncomplaining. He may even be rewarded with a degree of approval from his parents, who will be relieved that he is giving up his infantile needs and "growing up". He learns that there is a greater possibility of feeling valued when he behaves like a "little man" rather than displaying his age appropriate needs.

We can view this position of hopelessness as a secondary defence system, and it is a developmental achievement. It frequently occurs to me that my dismissing clients are very bright and appear to have been so from early in life. Intelligence and academic achievement are usually valued highly in their families, but it is also possible that advanced cognitive abilities are useful in holding oneself together from quite early in childhood. One dismissing person told me that she remembered the moment she decided she would never again trust her mother. She was four years old at the time. These young children may turn to books, or to mathematics, or collecting objects or facts in order to soothe themselves from the natural anxieties of feeling insecure.

Based on the work of Bick, Maggie Turp writes about the development of certain kinds of "psychic skin" to contain the self. Of particular relevance here is:

> the formation of a 'second skin' via 'skin toughening', a 'rhinoceros hide' defence that wards off fears of disintegration by forming a tough, impermeable barrier around the self. Where toughening becomes entrenched, dependence on attachment figures is replaced by pseudo-independence.
>
> (Turp, 2012, p. 68)

This "skin defence" may appear to provide immunity from narcissistic wounds, and indeed there are some avoidant individuals who also rely on grandiose inflation of the self and denigration of the other as a further layer of protection. This may be sufficient armour to keep shame from leaking out, and to prevent narcissistic wounding seeping in. For most, however, the pseudo-independence is built on very shaky foundations and under extreme duress they can crumble, revealing the core of ambivalent, preoccupied attachment needs.

A little more about Wes: unresolved trauma

As I have stated, the development of certain defences is adaptive. However, there are circumstances when the resultant impact on personality and functioning is so extreme, and has such serious implications, that it is termed psychopathy.

Wes, introduced earlier, showed evidence of typical avoidant traits but also ticked many of the boxes for unresolved trauma. (We must remember that "unresolved in respect of trauma or loss" is a *secondary* classification, always given in conjunction with either a core dismissing or preoccupied classification. Just occasionally there could be a pairing of secure-autonomous with "unresolved", following a recent traumatic event or major bereavement, but this may be a transient state rather than a defining trait.) It is hardly surprising given the extremes of neglect, abuse, and cruelty in his early relational environment that Wes's defences were extreme, brittle, and unstable, with a marked reliance on dissociation.

> As a result of … severe misattunement, the infant is left for long periods in an intensely disorganized psychobiological state that is beyond his or her coping strategies. The infant's response to such a fear-inducing environment consists of hyper-vigilance and hyper-arousal, followed by hypo-arousal or dissociation, which involves numbing, avoidance, compliance and restricted affect.
> (Renn, 2006, p. 61)

This combination of a dismissing core pattern of attachment with the disorganised features of complex post-traumatic stress disorder (Herman, 1992) is familiar to forensic staff working with violent offenders who also have a psychiatric illness or personality disorder. Lorenzini and Fonagy (2013) remind us that: "the hypoactivation of attachment shown by dismissing individuals is associated with schizoid, narcissistic, antisocial, and paranoid PDs [personality disorders]" (p. 161).

Researching the histories of Section 53 offenders (juveniles serving custodial sentences for violent crimes), Boswell (1995) found evidence of physical, sexual, emotional, or ritual abuse, along with loss and neglect in 91 per cent of the 200 cases studied. This was documented in official records (medical, educational, social services, family court, etc.) or personally reported.

Perhaps it is to be expected that we find trauma in the background of individuals who inflict trauma on others. de Zulueta explored these connections from an attachment perspective in her book *From Pain to Violence* (1993). But why is there a higher prevalence among serious offenders of a dismissing attachment pattern? Pointing out that both dismissing and unresolved patterns are found in higher proportions among offenders than in the general population, Adshead (2004) suggests that the inhibition of emotions and difficulty with empathy that are features of avoidant attachment are prerequisites to violently assaulting the body of another human being. In addition, "the reduced capacity to mentalise, to picture the mental states of the other, reduces inhibition of aggression by representing the victim as devoid of thoughts, feelings and the capacity for real suffering" (Fonagy and

Target, 1995, p. 489). Yet the victim is also perceived as a threat, perhaps challenging or humiliating the perpetrator.

> [For] psychopaths the experience of parenting or early life is so traumatising for the child that a defensive, violent and macho 'shell' is built up which maintains an illusion that the individual simply does not need anyone. ... [However] development offers opportunities as well as risks, so that the proto-psychopath will experience a series of opportunities to change – to become attached to objects who will not abuse. These invitations to intimacy will themselves become a threat, which needs to be ruthlessly put down.
> (Parker and Morris, 2004, pp. 197–198)

Although by no means a "psychopath", I suspect that Wes had developed a "macho shell" as a desperate defence against the humiliation, shame, and rage he felt, particularly in relation to his mother. Later, the masculine environment of military service felt containing with its discipline, routines, and rules, but romantic relationships were altogether more challenging, evoking his disavowed dependency needs. He wanted a relationship but, with his fragile sense of self and brittle defences, could not tolerate any challenge or threat, particularly from a woman. He felt intruded upon by the demands of his partner for attention, but also rejected when she told him to leave; under the influence of alcohol he lost control of his rage and lashed out.

John Bowlby's seminal paper on the relational backgrounds of young offenders, "Forty-four juvenile thieves: Their characters and home-life", was published in 1944. All these children, aged from six to sixteen, stole repeatedly, but fourteen of them stood out because of a particular quality to their personalities that Bowlby referred to as "affectionless" – they appeared detached, cold, and without emotion. These are features of a certain kind of dismissing attachment pattern also linked to psychopathy. He concluded that a combination of abuse, neglect, and separation had interfered with these children's normal development, in particular the establishment of a superego – a moral compass that inhibits antisocial impulses.

I met Wes many years after he was released from prison, and for most of that time he had attended Alcoholics Anonymous groups with their emphasis on accepting responsibility for actions that have caused pain to others. My sense of him was that he did have a highly functioning superego, albeit a self-critical, self-punishing one. It was hard for him to bear the memory of hitting his partner. I know that his shame about it had resulted in suicide attempts in the past and he now wanted to make restitution in some way. He often talked in therapy about his wish to be useful, to study or train in a profession where he could make a contribution to society. I was moved by his strong desire to make amends and earn a place for himself in the world, but this was in tension with the impulse to self-punishment. He had served his custodial term but appeared committed to the idea of a lifelong self-imposed sentence. We were able to do some work identifying how he might atone – for the assault, for the murderous feelings he still harboured toward his attachment figures, and for the "original sin" of having been born. However, he did not believe he could ever risk getting close to a woman again. Our relationship was a challenge to him, though one he chose for himself.

The intransigent nature of defences

Tirril Harris looked at how experiences with caregivers in early life are internalised to form internal working models. Where parental figures provide consistent, reliable responses to a child's attachment-eliciting communications, this is likely to form the core of secure attachment. Where caregiving and responsiveness is unreliable, the resultant pattern is typically preoccupied or enmeshed, and where caregiving is not only unreliable but abusive or frightening, we are likely to find disorganised or unresolved attachment. However, for those who develop an avoidant or dismissing pattern of attachment, the likely scenario is of *consistent* lack of response (or reliably consistent angry, rejecting responses) to the child's needs by parents (Harris, 2004).

I believe that this very consistency explains the avoidant client's entrenched defences and resistance to change. There may have been few opportunities with other caregivers to experience anything other than rejection, criticism, and injunctions to contain distress, with the overriding message not to expect help from anybody. He has adapted perfectly to his relational environment, and as internal working models influence how he views the world and other people, it seems absurd to make himself vulnerable to further rejection or attacks.

This is one reason why we see fewer dismissing clients seeking therapy than clients from the other insecure groups.

Shame

Another reason why an avoidant individual may shun therapeutic help is the dread of revealing himself to another person. The effects of narcissistic wounds are low self-esteem, self-contempt, and shame. As Mollon (1993) recognises: "Shame has a great deal to do with looking and being looked at" (p. 47). The gaze of another can re-evoke feelings and memories that are crippling. There may be an expectation that the other person will be cold, unempathic, or critical, just as earlier attachment figures were. Closeness with others, and perhaps particularly with a therapist, risks being exposed as an inadequate fraud. Better to feel contempt for any form of intimate relating than risk a traumatic exposé.

Regarding therapy, there may also be a fantasy of a warm, attuned, kindly psychotherapist and this could be equally disquieting for an avoidant client, opening up shameful longing and emotions that can't be controlled. A further aspect of resistance to therapy is a strong attachment to internal objects with critical parental voices. If an individual feels unwanted, unloved, and unlovable, he may turn against himself, tormenting himself with thoughts of his own inadequacy, and although the scars are not visible on his body these attacks cause as much pain as a knife wound. He feels contempt for himself, believing that he deserves to suffer, and this prevents him hoping for anything better. Indeed, this self-inflicted emotional pain may be needed in order to feel *something*. The wish is to not be seen, and for this sadomasochistic relationship with the self to remain a private affair. In not wanting anybody to interfere in his "bondage to bad objects" he is committed to not benefitting from anything good that comes his way. His refusal to take in, absorb, and be nourished by anything positive is a form of "relational anorexia".

Attitudes to therapy

> Evidence shows that these states of mind [unconscious distrust and evasion] occur especially in those who, having developed an anxiously avoidant pattern of attachment during early years, have striven ever since to be emotionally self-contained and insulated against intimate contact with other people. These patients, who are often described as being narcissistic or as having a false self, avoid therapy as long as they can and, should they undertake it, keep the therapist at arm's length.
>
> (Bowlby, 1988/1993, p. 143)

While private consulting rooms and National Health Service psychological therapy services (especially the higher intensity provision under the Increasing Access to Psychological Therapies programme) attract preoccupied clients and those with unresolved trauma, dismissing individuals are not necessarily beating their way to our consulting room doors. There are a number of reasons for this, including the tendency to minimise distress.

I have already explored why disdain or contempt are used as defences against a certain kind of intimacy that exists in the consulting room. Avoidant individuals experience depression, anxiety, loss, stress, and all of the life struggles that therapy can be helpful for, but the highly defended individual looks for other options. In general, self-help is more acceptable and in keeping with the injunction to be self-sufficient. There are many resources available on the internet, as well as apps and books that address symptom relief and promote wellbeing (see also Cundy, 2015).

If it is essential to engage with a therapist, help may be sought online where anonymity is maintained, or where it is possible to remain invisible or remote. I worked for, and was then Chair of, Hackney Bereavement Service, where we established an online project with counselling offered via real-time online messaging. Many of the clients who took this option rather than face-to-face sessions commented that they were able to express themselves more openly than would otherwise be comfortable; the invisibility and absence of vocal cues made it possible to feel safe, and even intimately connected to the counsellor whose responsive face they would never see. Counter to our expectations, online counselling was not used as a first step leading to face-to-face individual or group therapy.

If online counselling does not suit, approaches such as cognitive behavioural or solution-focused therapy may appeal, with their focus on thought processes and problem solving rather than relationship and emotional catharsis. They usually have the added advantage of being time-limited, discouraging dependency. Another possibility is life or executive coaching, often centred on workplace difficulties. These models are mostly prospective, looking to the future rather than exploring the past.

One long-term, open-ended approach that does seem to attract some dismissing individuals is formal psychoanalysis. I imagine it appeals as an intellectual exercise, where insight may be gained at a theoretical level, but those patients who are skilful in these things can evade genuine emotional engagement. It may also have the value of status, a luxury that can be afforded by the wealthy and successful, thus stoking defensive narcissism. While the stereotypical "blank screen analyst" may feel threatening to some, representing a silent, tight-lipped critical parent, she could also be cast in the role of a mere employee who simply provides an environment where the dismissing patient analyses himself, or as an intellectual equal with whom stimulating conversation is possible. This intellectual defence is a challenge for the psychoanalyst to grapple with.

Yet there are avoidant individuals who find their way to the kind of relational therapy that addresses the impact of early experiences on relationships with other people and with themselves. Many of the anxieties I have already mentioned are likely to be present. Alongside an expectation that the therapist will be critical, or intrusive, or demanding, may be a deeply buried longing to be seen and accepted. Alongside the fear that therapy will be exposing, shaming, or useless, there is a hope that maybe the client has at last found a safe haven.

Presentation in therapy

Therapeutic boundaries

For individuals with an armour-like psychic skin, the therapeutic "rules of engagement" provide a welcome structure to manage intimacy. In fact, a client's attitude to therapeutic boundaries is almost diagnostic of attachment style. While preoccupied and unresolved clients struggle to be contained within the boundaries, dismissing patients observe the rules carefully. They would be ashamed to arrive early and will leave promptly, often checking their watches during sessions if there is no clock in view. If an avoidant client is late for a session he will usually indicate that there are other commitments that are more important to him. As therapists, we may see something else at play, an anxiety about becoming attached or having revealed too much, and thus he regulates the intimacy by backing off a little.

The avoidant client does not miss us when we take a break! It is a relief to have more time to work, and to have a break himself from paying for this "self-indulgent luxury". However, he does tend to pay the full fee, and usually pays promptly. Payment underscores that this is a professional contract rather than a personal relationship, and it would be humiliating to negotiate a reduced fee, exposing the urgency of his need. He may also fear that a reduced fee puts him in our debt in some regard, making him vulnerable to being manipulated by us.

The avoidant individual in therapy does not appear to be interested in the therapist as a person, only in her function. He would not dream of asking personal questions but may establish a ritual of polite conversation at the start of sessions as evidence of his impeccable manners. He will rarely make contact between sessions other than to reschedule if absolutely necessary, and probably prefers to do this by email or text rather than telephone, as this is considered too intrusive.

So, dismissing clients are often viewed as "no trouble at all", although they may also be difficult to engage, to empathise with, or to hold onto. If they do settle into open-ended therapy, in my experience they are less likely to be taken to supervision than the more florid and demanding preoccupied clients or the chaotic, worrying unresolved ones.

Transference

Describing "narcissistic" analysands, Freud wrote: "They manifest no transference and for that reason are inaccessible to our efforts and cannot be cured by us" (1916–1917/1991, p. 500). As I have already mentioned, dismissing clients may appear to perceive the therapist as more or less irrelevant, simply there to provide the space in which the client can "analyse" himself. From an attachment perspective, however, we can easily see how this is congruent with his need to defend himself, and it is our responsibility to help him engage with therapy and make a trusting relationship with us.

It may be more acceptable to the client to "consult an expert" rather than to need therapy. One of my more avoidant clients likes to refer to me as "Doc" or "Prof" – although this is done with a humour that serves relationship. Almost the opposite is also found, where the therapist is viewed as incompetent, ridiculous, an intellectual inferior: "*Why on earth do you keep banging on about my childhood – that has nothing to do with anything*" or "*That's not what Freud said in his 1923 paper – haven't you even read it?*". These attacks on our competence can be hard to bear, and we need to remind ourselves that the more extreme the defence, the greater the underlying fear.

Other common transference manifestations are the therapist cast as benign but ineffectual – evidence of the client's resistance and "attachment to bad objects" – or the therapist "used" as a critical, demanding, shaming, or intrusive parent.

Countertransference

Dismissing clients can make us feel clumsy, deskilled, inarticulate, or inadequate. We can find ourselves trying to batter their defences by interrogating, firing questions at them, or attempting to outwit them. While some are undemanding and well behaved, we may dread sessions with others who bully or ridicule us, leaving us feeling humiliated. On the receiving end of frequent provocation, we may be drawn into retaliating, even ending the therapy. This, of course, confirms the patient's view that therapy is pointless, and his belief that nobody is willing to tolerate and understand his aggression has been proven. Josephine Klein wrote of the inestimable value of "holding by endurance" (1995), and Winnicott (1962) refers to the importance of not retaliating to provocations.

With the absence of affect in sessions, we may begin to feel irritated, bored, or disengaged. Possibilities for exploration can be scuppered by the client's anxiety about what might be opened up, so all of our attempts to engage with the material are blocked. This can also feel excruciatingly uncomfortable. Or we may discover that we are unable to hold these clients in mind: "The therapist may feel she and the patient are warily circling one another; the sessions may seem vacuous and difficult to recall afterward when writing notes" (Holmes, 1996, p. 25). We have clearly been drawn into a repetition, recalling the parents' inability to attune, to notice, or to hold the child in mind.

Unless we are particularly attuned, we may not recognise the signs of a developing attachment, evidence that we matter to our avoidant patients, and expect them to terminate therapy. I work with a number of people who have stayed for long-term psychotherapy, yet I still feel surprised when the doorbell rings at the start of each session. They are extraordinarily skilled at concealing their attachment to me. One clue that usually slips through is that I have very warm feelings for each of them. Several years into one therapy I teased one client saying, "I can't believe you don't think of me between sessions! Surely I'm memorable enough!".

Sometimes we feel emotions including anger, grief, fear, and delight that the client cannot allow. The shifting countertransference is, of course, valuable information. These individuals were probably unable to express their feelings or needs directly, and a therapist who is sensitive to this level of communication provides a new experience of attunement. On occasions we may find an image or fantasy coming to mind on behalf of the client. I worked with a young woman who presented as "untouchable" yet I often imagined myself stroking her hair, a soothing maternal gesture. I believe I was picking up her secret "shameful" longing to be cared for.

Defences in sessions

While the therapist works hard to attune, to make a connection, and to invite the client to open up, the client is likely to experience a split. The desire and hope that brought him to therapy is activated, but we are taking him into risky territory and his self-protective mechanisms are ready to kick in when he starts to feel too exposed – or if his attachment needs are activated. One tactic is to block memories, withhold feelings, downplay the impact of events, and maintain an idealisation of relationships or situations that were clearly suboptimal. Another is to fill the session with chatter in order to control the therapist; if we are not permitted to contribute to sessions then the therapy cannot be effective and the client can leave with his low expectations confirmed.

Dismissing clients may avoid discomfort by retreating into intellectualisation, or withdrawing into an adversarial silence. They may demand solutions to problems, not because they are unable to resolve these themselves, but to divert attention from their own affective state in the moment. I am sure we are all familiar with the use of humour as a distraction. Humour can be very helpful when working with dismissing individuals, but with the intention of making an intimate connection rather than avoidance. Clients may evade questions, change the subject, or be so lifeless and superficial that the therapist feels bored and despairing. All these and many more diversionary tactics mark the spot where anxiety has kicked in and pain is buried. The greater the defence, the stronger the underlying shame and fear that the client needs to disavow. This can of course be worked with. However, if we push too hard the ultimate defence is to miss sessions or terminate therapy.

Aims of psychotherapy

The overarching aim of all attachment-based psychotherapy is to help our patients, whatever their core pattern of attachment, to become more secure and resilient, to create healthier relationships with other people and with themselves, and to bring about changes in their internal worlds that impact on their external lives. The defining qualities of secure adults have been identified by extensive research, including the AAI, and contemporary attachment theory also contributes to our understanding of secure and insecure ways of being. We know, for instance, that secure-autonomous adults are characterised by their balanced, coherent narrative style (for a good overview, see Main *et al.*, 2008), their capacity to mentalise (e.g. Bouchard *et al.*, 2008; Fonagy *et al.*, 1998; Hobson, 2004), and by their ability to regulate their affective states without resorting to either hypo- or hyper-activation (e.g. Cozolino, 2006; Schore, 2003a, 2003b). We can make use of this knowledge to guide our interventions over the life of a psychotherapy. Specific techniques are not required, though sometimes these may be helpful.

This is not a formulaic, manualised approach but a deeply relational one. The emphasis is likely to shift between these areas of focus within sessions and over time, but in a successful therapy they will all be addressed at some point. Creating a meaningful narrative gives perspective on life's difficulties but may not help the client to let go of harsh self-criticism; the development of self-awareness and understanding are necessary, but need to be complemented by the emotional work of grieving.

The early phase

Avoidant clients are wary of dependency or being trapped, so the offer of a few sessions initially can feel more welcoming, an opportunity to make an informed decision about whether the experience is useful before making a bigger commitment.

During those early sessions, the client's attitude to therapy and therapeutic boundaries, his narrative style and evidence of defences, and the therapist's countertransference responses will either support or disconfirm the initial formulation of attachment pattern. While familiarising herself with the context of the client's life, the therapist looks to introduce him to the experience of therapy. It is less threatening to focus on a current or recent difficulty outside the consulting room and use this as an example of how psychotherapy works, exploring what happened, how the client responded, how he felt, and his need to protect himself from feeling more angry or upset. Opportunities may arise to examine how he reacts to stress so that patient and therapist can think together about better strategies. In other words, it is vital to communicate that the patient's defences are respected.

In the first few sessions we usually hear the client's attacks on, and unrealistic expectations of, himself. It may be possible to point these out – as long as the client seems ready to be "seen" in this way and is prepared to explore his relationship with himself. This is a way in to his inner world and a foundation on which to begin the "work of feelings" once there is an agreement to longer-term or open-ended therapy. The focus in the early stages would be the client's relationships with other people currently in his life, and his relationship with his own internal world. Looking to the past, or acknowledging the therapeutic relationship, are often best left until trust has developed and once a decision has been made to continue. Transference interpretations, acknowledging that there is an "us", are likely to alienate a patient who is defended against intimacy. Harris cautions us against the premature assumption of a therapeutic relationship:

> for dismissive clients who have not yet built a working alliance the simple suggestion that a forthcoming break is likely to make them anxious, far from being enlightening, may alienate them not only from a particular psychotherapist, but from the therapy process altogether.
>
> (2004, p. 196)

Where therapeutic work must take place within a very brief time frame, it may be that this is all that can be achieved. However, a good experience for the client may encourage him to seek more in the future.

Specific areas of focus in therapy with dismissing clients

Bowlby writes that the aim of psychotherapy with "false self" individuals is: "To provide, *by being ourselves*, the conditions in which a patient of this kind can discover and recover what Winnicott calls his real self, and I call his attachment desires and feelings" (1988/1993, p. 57, my italics).

In order for a dismissing client to "earn" security, we need to help him develop similar capacities to those taken for granted by individuals who had the good fortune to benefit from a secure attachment history. It is particularly important when working with a highly defended individual to ensure that interventions do not risk shaming him.

Therapy should help him:

To notice: to observe himself and the relationship between his inner world, defences, and behaviour. Through developing an "observing ego", he can become familiar with his internal world and the memories, emotions, and fantasies he has distracted himself from. Remembering and exploring his dreams can be helpful to this process, as can reflecting on the relationship between "what goes on in here" – the consulting room – and "what goes on out there, in other kinds of relationships". This is linked to the capacity to mentalise, or reflective function (RF), although the latter is an implicit way of being rather than an explicit activity (actively noticing).

To feel: and to tolerate the full range and intensity of emotions. This requires attunement and therapeutic skill, to bring the client into relationship with the realm of emotions, to help him sit with unfamiliar and often painful feelings, to name them, and learn to be guided by them: "Assistance with experiencing increasing levels of positive and negative affect is a vital component of both parenting and psychotherapy" (Cozolino, 2002/2010, p. 23). We should remember that intense joy and excitement may also have been disavowed, and these also have a place in the consulting room. Humour and playfulness can help to access these more "positive" affects, though care must be taken to avoid shaming, intruding upon, or alienating the client.

To relate: to relax defensive boundaries between self and other, risk opening up and making meaningful contact, and creating moments of intimacy. Relating includes being prepared to ask for help from other people and from the therapist, and to accept help when offered. This is often challenging. It can be useful to identify someone in his life who can be "recruited", so he can practice revealing more of himself, risking more personal conversations, and inviting greater closeness. It is important, however, to be aware that interpersonal boundaries are sometimes necessary for self-protection.

In sessions, the therapist creates opportunities for affectively charged moments when both parties become aware of a bond existing between them. The timing of interventions is crucial, and evocative, emotion-rich words are chosen with the aim of reaching through the client's defensive shield in these moments. My own attitude to therapeutic boundaries is somewhat different when the client is avoidant: I actively invite contact between sessions when I am aware that he is coping with extra stress, knowing that my offer will rarely be accepted. However, should it ever be taken up I feel that we have made a breakthrough.

To mentalise: Adults rated secure-autonomous in the AAI have a far greater ability to reflect on, and to make sense of, the minds of other people than do insecure interviewees (Fonagy et al., 1998). The latter, including those rated dismissing, may be reluctant to wonder about what goes on in minds (including their own), or their perceptions may be very skewed. According to Fonagy and Target: "To some degree the avoidant child shuns the mental states of the other" (1998, p. 20) – it is painful to be confronted with the indifference, judgemental attitude, or disappointment they anticipate finding there.

> The person who is dismissing towards attachment-related experiences, the stiff-upper-lip type of individual, seems to have a constrained and in some ways impoverished relation to her own past. Much emotion seems to have been repressed or dealt with in other ways that make it unavailable for thought.
> (Hobson, 2004, pp. 178–179)

Psychotherapy aims to help clients not only to reflect on their mental activity, but also to make their once-repressed emotions available for reflection.

Expressing the central importance of mentalising to attachment-informed therapy, Holmes and Slade point out that: "Mentalising represents alexithymia's antithesis: the capacity to transform primitive impulses into feelings, and to represent, symbolise, sublimate, abstract, reflect, and make meaning of them" (2017, p. 68). Reflecting on conscious and unconscious motivations becomes second nature in time, a trait rather than a state, and implicit in this is the understanding that other people are similarly influenced by thoughts, feelings, memories, and fantasies. In other words, this marks a revision of internal working models, from insecure to more secure.

To create a meaningful self-narrative: narratives are emotionally informed stories that chart and make sense of the course of one's life. Secure-autonomous adults address painful life events and relational experiences through a balanced, considered, undefended narrative style. We try to help our avoidant clients do the same. I have previously suggested that the single most important question in psychotherapy is: "Why do you think your parents behaved as they did towards you when you were a child?" (Cundy, 2017). This is a question from the AAI that helps to indicate the interviewee's level of reflective functioning. Where reflective functioning is high, the client's response is likely to span several generations, recognising that his attachment figures' own experiences of being parented and the events and contexts of their lives before he was conceived shaped their fantasies and the needs they brought to their roles as parents. This, in turn, impacted on his early life and development and may also have influenced his relationship with his own children.

To recognise and mourn losses and deprivations: mourning has a key role in attachment-based therapy but denial, the foundation of the avoidant client's defences, makes it impossible to grieve for experiences of love and safety that were lost, or were never available. We need to find ways to undo denial so the client can confront the reality of his early life and begin to feel the unhappiness and anger he has evaded for so long. Specific memories of crushing experiences often emerge, accompanied by the feelings that had been detached and repressed. This is an important stage in the work. But mourning must eventually come to an end, making way for new possibilities and perspectives.

In the AAI, secure-autonomous interviewees' responses reveal that they "seem at ease with imperfections in the self. Relatedly, there is explicit or implicit forgiveness of/compassion for/acceptance of parents' failings" (Main et al., 2008 p. 57). While it is necessary for a dismissing client to acknowledge the impact of loss on his life, it is ultimately unhelpful, and often unfair, to continue raging about the failings of attachment figures. A new understanding needs to be found where parents are seen as individuals shaped by their own histories, social environment, and relational patterns. It may even become possible to remember times when they were more loving, or to recognise their valuable qualities.

To find compassion for himself as a child, and accept his "flaws" as an adult. This becomes possible when the client is able to grieve for what was missing in his early life.

> The person who is free to evaluate attachments is able to assimilate and think about her own past experiences in relationships, even when these have been unsatisfactory. She has mental space to relate to her own relations with others. She can reflect on her own feelings and impulses and can forgive and tolerate her own shortcomings.
> (Hobson, 2004, pp. 178–179)

Forgiving and tolerating one's shortcomings is a big step toward silencing self-punishing internal objects.

To challenge his continued attachment to punitive, critical internal objects, and resultant hidden self-harm. Miller recognised that childhood experiences with caregivers are internalised and, where these are unhappy, form the core of a harsh, punitive superego or relationship with the self: "The way we were treated as small children is the way we treat ourselves the rest of our life. And we often impose our most agonizing suffering upon ourselves. We can never escape the tormentor within ourselves" (1987, p. 133). Clearly, this dynamic must be challenged whenever it appears. A sadomasochistic relationship with oneself can have an addictive quality; self-inflicted but invisible emotional pain may be experienced as the only real feeling available to a highly constricted individual, and therapy can be scuppered if he is unwilling to "leave the relationship".

This has been the focus of Oliver's therapy for some time, and we often return to it. As noted earlier, he has a rich internal world but is often crushed by the vicious put-downs and insidious undermining by his "bad internal objects". These prevent him from making a satisfying life for himself, despite his many talents and lovely qualities. Early on, I encouraged him to notice when his "internal bully" was operating, and to tell me the kinds of messages he gives himself. I explored with him the origins of his oppressive relationship with himself – when he began to be self-critical, what were the circumstances, and how he felt at the time. I asked him how it has affected his life in the intervening years. He has become skilful at noticing the internal process operating and what triggers it.

I try to pick up on any evidence that a self-destructive dynamic is operating during sessions. I tell him: "You are living with a bully. If someone else treated you this way you could leave." I point out that he would never be so cruel to other people. I suggest that he is punishing himself for a perceived crime or unforgivable failure and I invite him to reflect on what it is about him that deserves such unkind treatment.

Oliver has come a long way in therapy and can often silence the internal put-downs now, but on occasions he still gives in to it. We have explored what he needs to do in order to earn release from his self-imposed prison. I have asked: "What kind of person do you aspire to be? What do you need to do to earn self-respect so you can stop tormenting yourself?". These kinds of interventions have a powerful effect, often enabling him to access sadness and grief.

To enjoy warmth, spontaneity, creativity, and connection – to come alive. Gerhardt refers to people with avoidant patterns as "low reactors". Not only do they down-regulate their emotional responses, it seems they also inhibit the absorption of cortisol.

> The switch into low cortisol mode also appears to be a kind of defence mechanism. It is an attempt at disengagement from painful feelings through avoidance, withdrawal and denial of painful experience ... better to feel nothing than to cope with relatively continuous painful experience.
>
> (2004, p. 80)

This can create chronic inhibition and a kind of low-level depression that needs to be countered. Clients register their therapists' affective states and energy levels, and we attempt to energise our exchanges through the tone, volume, speed, modulation, rhythm, and lyrical qualities of our voices, used to soothe or elevate mood. Likewise, we express our aliveness through the energy in our bodies: the speed and depth of breathing, the soft or sharp focus of eyes, animation of movement, gestures, and facial expressions in response to the client. Unlike the original attachment figures, "the therapist must be experienced as being in a state of *vitalizing attunement* to the patient" (Schore, 2003a, p. 279, my italics). Humour has an important place in therapy with avoidant patients, in the service of playfulness and relationship.

To install a new internal object that protects, supports, encourages, and celebrates him. This is the best protection against the assaults of a punitive superego. A new secure object can be constructed from the client's experiences in therapy: the therapist's genuine interest, care, and delight in him; her survival of his attacks; her efforts to protect him from attacks by his internal objects; and her efforts to create "moments of meeting" (Stern et al., 1998). The rhythms and particular rituals and culture that develop between client and therapist have a part to play. Being able to refer back to conversations or experiences shared in the past is evidence of holding each other in mind – "*Do you remember what you told me about your birth the first time we met?*"; "*I remember you telling me a similar dream a few years ago*"; or, "*I will never forget the expression on your face when I told you I was getting married – you looked genuinely happy for me.*"

We try to help the client introject the therapist, identify with her, and call upon this internal resource for help when needed – "*What would Linda say about this?*". We also encourage him to take seriously, to take in, and be nourished by the love, care, and respect of others rather than dismissing them or feeling too embarrassed to accept their affection graciously. It is also important to help him recognise the genuinely helpful efforts of his parents and other attachment figures, distinguishing between what they *did* (or didn't do) and what they *wanted to do* – but were unable. It may even be possible to create a new kind of adult–adult relationship with parents who are still alive (but not always). Risking opening up to others brings many rewards and these are also incorporated into the new "internal secure object".

At a recent session with a long-term dismissing client she told me: *"I felt overwhelmed with sadness but I knew this time would pass."*

A little more about Ayesha

When Ayesha (mentioned earlier) began her therapy with me, she told a story about her parents' lives before she was born. She recognised how difficult life had been for them in their country of origin, especially as their marriage was frowned on by their extended families, and they faced struggles as immigrants starting out in London. Because of this, she believed that she had made excessive and unreasonable demands, especially on her mother. In her world-view, she had been a greedy, messy, demanding child whose parents had done their best. After many years in psychotherapy she sees things slightly differently. While still feeling empathy for her parents, she eventually felt angry at the pressures and restrictions they imposed on her and her siblings and began to hold them responsible for the choices they had made. The extent of the emotional deprivation she had suffered in her well-to-do, immaculate home with an ambitious father and controlling mother became evident. She was able to cry as well as rage. She has begun to accept that her needs for affection and protection were normal, as was her need for her boundaries to be respected. However, she cannot yet acknowledge that she, like other children, needed her attachment figures to enjoy and delight in her; that thought is still too painful. Yet *I* enjoy and delight in her, and I'm sure she is aware of that.

Ayesha now lives with her partner and enjoys sharing her life with him. She misses him when he is away. She has a much healthier relationship with food, and with herself. However, accepting that contact with her parents continues to disturb her, she is careful to limit her communication with them. This is in the spirit of self-preservation. This woman, who was once anorexic regarding both food and relationships, has taken in and been nourished by good experiences with people, including myself, who genuinely care for her and with this new internal resource, and her capacity to self-reflect and mentalise, she is far more secure. Were she to take part in an AAI, I am confident that her transcript would now be assigned "secure-autonomous".

A few words about the avoidant psychotherapist

Discussions with students and colleagues over the years suggests that many people with a dismissing pattern of attachment may be drawn to the professions of counselling, psychotherapy, counselling psychology, and psychoanalysis. While it is assumed that our own therapy during training enables us to "earn" security, under strain our default position can emerge.

Attachment style may influence our choice of theoretical model and the setting we choose to work in. Some may prefer to work online, or with a brief model that does not require the development of a deep attachment to clients. Others are motivated by a longing to experience intimacy, but of a particular, manageable kind: the rather controlled intimacy of the 50-minute hour with its one-sided self-disclosure. For avoidant individuals, it is acceptable to be viewed as strong and dependable, to care for others rather than to seek care for themselves. Also, as previously explained, many have rich, if private, internal worlds and are therefore sensitive to others who are similarly narcissistically wounded and defended.

One danger may be that all of one's capacity for intimacy is invested in patients rather than personal relationships, and long working hours, including evenings and weekends, also minimise availability to family and loved ones. And, after so much time spent relating, the avoidant psychotherapist may need to retreat for a time to regroup.

It may be difficult for dismissing practitioners to accept that they matter to their clients, and important evidence to the contrary can be missed, especially when the client has a similar relational style. The impact of breaks on the client may be downplayed or overlooked. The therapeutic couple may collude to avoid painful feelings, keeping therapy at an intellectual level. These therapies may terminate early, and the ending process may be avoided by practitioners who are uncomfortable with expressions of both intimacy and distress.

When working with more preoccupied clients who tend to test boundaries, dismissing psychotherapists may feel intruded upon and become judgemental, with the danger of responding with an unempathic imposition of "rules". They may protect themselves from the urgency of the patients' needs, become cold and withholding, keeping the client at bay with interpretations.

However, the avoidant therapist is particularly astute and sensitive to the defensive manoeuvres of dismissing clients. Also, her capacity to think under pressure is a valuable tool, useful when under attack from dismissing clients, or in the presence of preoccupied clients' highly charged emotional states, or in the midst of traumatic re-enactments, chaos, and turmoil working with someone unresolved in respect of trauma. When this is matched with a capacity to feel deeply, to attune, and to empathise, we have the best of all worlds, an extraordinarily skilful psychotherapist.

Conclusion

In Dickens' *A Christmas Carol*, Ebenezer Scrooge is the archetypal avoidant character, shunning relationships with other people and with his internal world of painful memories. It is a wonderful, deeply psychological tale of redemption through confronting the pain of loss, separation, rejection, and cruelty. By isolating himself from the warmth of relationships Scrooge continues to torment himself, but his uncharacteristic concern for Tiny Tim, the fragile son of his clerk, Bob Cratchit, allows a route back to his own childhood. Following the therapeutic interventions of the three ghostly spirits of Christmas, he exclaims: "I will live in the Past, the Present, and the Future! The Spirits of all Three shall strive within me" (Dickens, 1843/2014, p. 59). It is a perfect parable of psychotherapy with avoidant patients.

Dismissing clients may evoke difficult feelings in the therapist, or may make little impact on the therapist's mind. If we can recognise the narcissistic wounding, the tragedy, and the shame that is so often disavowed, we can be more attuned and useful.

I conclude with a quotation, not from Bowlby but from Freud:

> The neurotic who is cured has really become another man, though at bottom, of course, he has remained the same; that is to say, he has become what he might have become at best under the most favourable conditions. But that is a very great deal.
> (1916–1917/1991, pp. 486–487)

In the language of attachment, he has earned security.

References

Adshead, G. (2004). Three degrees of security: Attachment and forensic institutions. In: F. Pfäfflin and G. Adshead (eds.), *A Matter of Security: The Application of Attachment Theory to Forensic Psychiatry and Psychotherapy* (pp. 147–166). London: Jessica Kingsley.

Bollas, C. (1987). *The Shadow of the Object: Psychoanalysis of the Unthought Known*. London: Free Association Books.

Boswell, G.R. (1995). *Violent Victims*. London: Prince's Trust.

Bouchard, M-A., Target, M., Lecours, S., Fonagy, P., Tremblay, L-M., Schachter, A., and Stein, H. (2008). Mentalization in adult attachment narratives: Reflective functioning, mental states, and affect elaboration compared. *Psychoanalytic Psychology*, 25, 47–66.

Bowlby, J. (1944). Forty-four juvenile thieves: Their characters and home-life. *International Journal of Psycho-Analysis*, 25, 107–128.

Bowlby, J. (1991). *Attachment and Loss, Volume 1: Attachment*. London: Penguin. (Original work published 1969).

Bowlby, J. (1993). *A Secure Base: Clinical Implications of Attachment Theory*. London: Routledge. (Original work published 1988).

Cozolino, L. (2006). *The Neuroscience of Human Relationships: Attachment and the Developing Social Brain*. New York: Norton.

Cozolino, L. (2010). *The Neuroscience of Psychotherapy: Healing the Social Brain*. New York: Norton. (Original work published 2002).

Cundy, L. (2015). Attachment, self-experience, and communication technology: Love in the age of the Internet. In: L. Cundy (ed.), *Love in the Age of the Internet: Attachment in the Digital Era* (pp. 1–29). London: Karnac.

Cundy, L. (2017). Fear of abandonment and angry protest: Understanding and working with anxiously attached clients. In: L. Cundy (ed.), *Anxiously Attached: Understanding and Working with Preoccupied Attachment* (pp. 19–48). London: Karnac.

de Zulueta, F. (1993). *From Pain to Violence: The Traumatic Roots of Destructiveness*. London: Whurr.

Dickens, C. (2014). *A Christmas Carol in Prose, Being a Ghost-Story of Christmas*. New York: Global Classics. (Original work published 1843).

Fairbairn, W.R.D. (1994). *Psychoanalytic Studies of the Personality*. London: Routledge. (Original work published 1952).

Fonagy, P. and Target, M. (1995). Understanding the violent patient: The use of the body and the role of the father. *International Journal of Psycho-Analysis*, 76, 487–501.

Fonagy, P. and Target, M. (1998). An interpersonal view of the infant. In: A. Hurry (ed.), *Psychoanalysis and Developmental Therapy* (pp. 3–31). London: Karnac.

Fonagy, P., Target, M., Steele, H., and Steele, M. (1998). Reflective-functioning manual, Version 5.0, for application to Adult Attachment Interview. Unpublished research manual, University College London.

Freud, A. (1993) *The Ego and the Mechanisms of Defence*. London: Karnac. (Original work published 1936).

Freud, S. (1916–1917) *Introductory Lectures on Psycho-Analysis*, S.E., 16. London: Hogarth Press. Reprinted 1991, London: Penguin.

Gerhardt, S. (2004). *Why Love Matters: How Affection Shapes a Baby's Brain.* Hove, UK: Brunner-Routledge.
Greenfield, S. (2008). *ID: The Quest for Meaning in the 21st Century.* London: Hodder & Stouton.
Greenfield, S. (2015). *Mind Change: How Digital Technologies are Leaving Their Mark on Our Brains.* London: Rider.
Harris, T. (2004). Chef or chemist? Practicing psychotherapy within the attachment paradigm. *Attachment and Human Development, 6* (2), 191–207.
Her (2013). Film, directed by Spike Jonze. USA: Warner Bros.
Herman, J.L. (1992). *Trauma and Recovery: From Domestic Violence to Political Terror.* New York: Basic Books.
Hobson, P. (2004). *The Cradle of Thought: Exploring the Origins of Thinking.* Oxford: Oxford University Press.
Holmes, J. (1996). *Attachment, Intimacy, Autonomy: Using Attachment Theory in Adult Psychotherapy.* Northvale, NJ: Aronson.
Holmes, J. (2001). *The Search for the Secure Base: Attachment Theory and Psychotherapy.* Hove, UK: Routledge.
Holmes, J. and Slade, A. (2017). *Attachment in Therapeutic Practice.* London: Sage.
Klein, J. (1995). *Doubts and Certainties in the Practice of Psychotherapy.* London: Karnac.
Lorenzini, N. and Fonagy, P. (2013). Attachment and personality disorders: A short review. *FOCUS: The Journal of Lifelong Learning in Psychiatry, 11*(2), 155–166.
Main, M. and Weston, D.R. (1982). Avoidance of the attachment figure in infancy: Descriptions and interpretations. In: C. Murray Parkes and J. Stevenson-Hinde (eds.), *The Place of Attachment in Human Behavior* (pp. 31–59). New York: Basic Books.
Main, M., Hesse, E., and Goldwyn, R. (2008). Studying differences in language usage in recounting attachment history: An introduction to the AAI. In: H. Steele and M. Steele (eds.), *Clinical Applications of the Adult Attachment Interview* (pp. 31–68). New York: Guilford.
Miller, A. (1987). *For Your Own Good: The Roots of Violence in Child-Rearing.* London: Virago. (Original work published 1980).
Mitchell, S.A. and Black, M.J. (1995). *Freud and Beyond.* New York: Basic Books.
Mollon, P. (1993). *The Fragile Self: The Structure of Narcissistic Disturbance.* London: Whurr.
Mollon, P. (2002). *Shame and Jealousy: The Hidden Turmoils.* London: Karnac.
Parker, M. and Morris, M. (2004). Finding a secure base: Attachment in Grendon Prison. In: F. Pfäfflin and G. Adshead (eds.), *A Matter of Security: The Application of Attachment Theory to Forensic Psychiatry and Psychotherapy* (pp. 193–207). London: Jessica Kingsley.

Power, A. and Cundy, L. (2015). Net gains and losses: Digital technology and the couple. In: L. Cundy (ed.), *Love in the Age of the Internet: Attachment in the Digital Era* (pp. 53–80). London: Karnac.

Renn, P. (2006). Attachment, trauma and violence: Understanding destructiveness from an attachment theory perspective. In: C. Harding (ed.), *Aggression and Destructiveness: Psychoanalytic Perspectives* (pp. 57–78). London: Routledge.

Robertson, J. and Robertson, J. (1969). *Young Children in Brief Separations: John, 17 months; 9 days in a residential nursery*. Film series, Tavistock Institute, London.

Schore, A.N. (2003a). *Affect Regulation and the Repair of the Self*. New York: Norton.

Schore, A.N. (2003b). *Affect Dysregulation and Disorders of the Self*. New York: Norton.

Spencer, H. (1864). *The Principles of Biology, Volume 1*. London: Williams & Norgate.

Steiner, J. (1993). *Psychic Retreats: Pathological Organizations in Psychotic, Neurotic and Borderline Patients*. Hove, UK: Routledge.

Stern, D.N., Sander, L.W., Nahum, J.P., Harrison, A.M., Lyons-Ruth, K., Morgan, A.C., Bruschweiler-Stern, N., and Tronick, E.Z. (1998). Non-interpretive mechanisms in psychoanalytic therapy: The 'something more' than interpretation (The Process of Change Study Group). *International Journal of Psycho-Analysis, 79*, 903–921.

Tronick, E. (2007). *Neurobehavioral and Social Emotional Development of Infants and Children*. New York: Norton.

Tronick, E., Als, H., Adamson, L., and Brazelton, T. (1978). The infant's response to entrapment between contradictory messages in face-to-face interaction. *Journal of the American Academy of Child Psychiatry, 17*, 1–13.

Turp, M. (2003). *Hidden Self-Harm: Narratives from Psychotherapy*. London: Jessica Kingsley.

Turp, M. (2012). Clinging on for dear life: Adhesive identification and experience in the countertransference. *British Journal of Psychotherapy, 28*(1): 66–80.

Turkle, S. (2005). *The Second Self: Computers and the Human Spirit*. Cambridge, MA: MIT Press.

Turkle, S. (2011). *Alone Together: Why We Expect More from Technology and Less From Each Other*. New York: Basic Books.

Williams, G. (2002). *Internal Landscapes and Foreign Bodies: Eating Disorders and Other Pathologies*. London: Karnac. (Original work published 1997).

Winnicott, D.W. (1960). Ego distortion in terms of true and false self. In: D.W. Winnicott (1965), *The Maturational Processes and the Facilitating Environment* (pp. 140–152). London: Hogarth Press.

Winnicott, D.W. (1962). The aims of psycho-analytical treatment. In: D.W. Winnicott (1965), *The Maturational Processes and the Facilitating Environment* (pp. 166–170). London: Hogarth Press.

INDEX

AAI (Adult Attachment Interview) xiv, 24–28, 79–80, 99
adaptation of infants to parents 1, 10, 38, 70–73, 77–78, 89; as skill 73–74
addiction 44, 52; *see also* alcohol, drugs and avoidance
Adshead, G. 87
Adult Attachment Interview (AAI) xiv, 24–28, 79–80, 99
affairs 53–54, 84
Ainsworth, M.D.S. 16, 23
alcohol, drugs and avoidance 42, 49, 79
alexithymia *see* body signals and emotions
Alvarez, A. 2, 10
ambivalent attachment *see* preoccupied (enmeshed) personalities
angry-dismissive insecure styles 26, 27, 33
Anna (adult, withdrawn attachment) 28–32, 81
appearance (physical) as defence 81–82
approval/disapproval by parents 72, 82, 85; *see also* Ayesha

asceticism as defence 80–81, 83; *see also* Ayesha
ASI (Attachment Style Interview) xiv, 25–28, 28–29, 30–33
attachment theory xv–xvi, 23, 28, 48, 70–72, 80, 96
attachment, tools for measuring 24–28
avoidance: degrees of 72–74; styles of 24, 26–28, 41–42
avoidant/ambivalent (preoccupied) couples: misattunement in 1–2, 38, 45, 48, 51–55; in therapy 55–56, 59–63
avoidant/avoidant couples 48–49, 52
avoidant/disorganised couples 49
Ayesha (adult, no-entry defence) 76–78, 83, 103

Bartholomew, K. 41, 42
Biographical Narrative Interview Method 33
Black, M.J. 78
blind babies, developing responsiveness in 5

boarding school and attachment avoidance xiii–xiv, 1–2, 44
body signals and emotions: clients' awareness of 2, 16–18; in therapy 39–40, 42, 57, 58
Bollas, C. 7
Boswell, G.R. 87
Bowlby, John: on attachment needs and developing detachment 37, 39, 45, 71, 88; on observable behaviour 25, 27, 28; on research xvi, 23, 33–34; on therapy 31, 64, 90, 97, 105
brain functioning and emotions 16–18, 45
Bullock, R. 32

care-giving and care-seeking and avoidant attachment 40, 51, 52, 53, 64, 104; and secure attachment 45–47, 60
caregivers *see* children; mothers
Castellano, R. 39, 46, 47
Cheryl (adult, false positivity) 43, 57
children: adapting to parental demands 1, 10, 38, 70–73, 77–78, 89; avoiding intrusion 82–83; conditions for optimal development 9–10; downplaying own emotional needs 15–16, 39, 41, 85; neglect in therapy xiii, 8, 18–19; rationalising parental behaviour 80
circular questions in therapy 61–63
cleanliness as defence 76, 79
closeness *see* intimacy (closeness)
Clulow, C. 41
compassion, developing 63, 64, 100
compliant defences xiii, 55–56, 58
Connors, M.E. 58–59
Conterio, K. 30
Cooper, A.M. 31
cortisol levels 101–102
countertransference: challenges posed by xiii, xiv, 2–4, 8, 19, 94–95; used in therapy 96; *see also* therapists, personal attachment style
couple relationships: balancing intimacy and distance 38–39, 44–45, 52; care-giving and care-seeking 45–47, 50–51, 64; challenges faced in 53–55; choosing a partner and forming attachment 48–51; and therapy 46, 54–56, 59–63
Crittenden, P.M. 41
culture and attachment xv, 2, 9, 43–45, 50, 70, 73
Cundy, L. xiii, xv–xvi, 29

Dallos, R. 33
Damasio, A.R. 17
Davis, K.E. 54
de Zulueta, F. 87
defences: adaptive value of xvi, 47, 73, 86, 89; definition 1, 69, 70–71; secondary 85–86; and therapy 55–59, 63, 91–96, 97–98; various types of 17, 78–83
denial as defence 46, 54, 79–80, 83, 100, 102; *see also* Lucy
depression and avoidant individuals 27, 53, 57, 91, 102
DeWall, C.N. 54
digital era, connecting in xvi, 44–45, 52, 54, 84–85, 91
disapproval *see* approval/disapproval by parents
dismissing attachment personalities: characteristics of 16, 26, 27, 33, 41, 73, 85–86; childhood development of 38, 39, 89; in couple relationships 40–41, 44–45, 46–49, 51–55, 84–85; therapists with 59, 104–105; in therapy 42–43, 58, 59–63, 69, 90–95, 97–103; *see also* Ayesha; Lucy; Oliver; Wes
disorganised/unresolved attachment styles 24, 26, 49, 87, 89
divorce 54–55
drugs, alcohol and avoidance 42, 49, 79

EFCT (Emotion Focused Couple Therapy) 55, 60–61
Emanuel, L. 8
embedded research 32
Emde, R.N. 10
Emotion Focused Couple Therapy (EFCT) 55, 60–61

emotions and the body *see* body signals and emotions
empathy: and brain 17–18; in couples 47, 53, 56, 61; lack of 7, 72, 87; in therapy with avoidant clients 8, 19, 58, 69, 93, 104–105
enactments in therapy 2, 8, 9, 30–31, 61, 62
enmeshed insecure styles *see* preoccupied (enmeshed) personalities
Ezquerro, A. 31

Fairbairn, W.R.D. 80
false self: developing and maintaining 32, 41, 45, 64, 70, 79; in therapy 43, 55–56, 90, 97
Farnfield, S. 25
Favazza, A.R. 30
fearful insecure/avoidant styles 26, 27, 41
Finzi, R. 55
Fiona (adult, defensive devaluing) 42–43
Fonagy, P. 87, 99
forgiveness: for caregivers 80, 99–100, 102–103, 103; for self 100–101
Fraiberg, Selma 5
Freud, Anna 80–81
Freud, Sigmund 14, 29, 93, 105

gay couples 52
Gazzaniga, Michael 17
Gender 52
Gerhardt, S. 101
Gina and Sam (avoidant/preoccupied couple) 55–56, 62–63

Hackney Bereavement Service 91
Harris, T. 32–33, 89, 97
Hazan, C. 50
Henry, Gianna 8
Her (film) 85
Hill, K. 33
Hobson, P. 99, 100
Holmes, J. 26, 49, 71, 73, 94, 99
hopelessness and avoidant individuals 37, 60, 85–86
Horowitz, L.M. 41, 42
humour: as defence 79, 81; in therapy 93, 95, 98, 102

idealisation: of self 41–42; of significant others 59, 95
independence *see* self-sufficiency
inhibition *see* repression/inhibition as defence
internal working models 28, 39, 41, 45, 48, 89, 99
internet, and relationships xvi, 44–45, 52, 54, 84–85, 91
interoception 2
intimacy (closeness) and avoidant attachment 26, 31–32, 80–81; and avoidant therapist 104; and couple relationships 39, 46–49, 56; definition 64; and friendship 83; and sex 42, 52; and technology 44, 84–85; and therapy 43, 61, 90–91, 92–93, 97, 98
intrusive/withdrawn mothers xvi, 16, 18, 41, 43, 73, 82–83
investment theory 54

John, film of baby 71
Johnson, S.M. 60
Jonze, Spike (filmmaker) 85
Josh (avoidant child) and countertransference 3–4
Jung, C.G. 48

King, Frederic Truby (pedagogue) 72
Kirkpatrick, L.A. 54
Klein, J. 94
Klein, M. 29

Lorenzini, N. 87
love, falling in 48, 50
Lucy (teenager, deactivated attachment) 10–17

McDougall, J. 8
McGilchrist, I. 17
Main, M. 72, 100
mate selection and attachment 48–51
mentalising 12, 46, 87–88, 96, 98–99, 100
Mike (adult, dismissing avoidant, longing to be seen) 37–38, 39–40, 43, 56–58
Mikulincer, M. 41, 58

Miller, A. 71, 100–101
mistrust/trust: and avoidance 10, 26, 31, 41, 90; in therapy 77, 93, 97
Mitchell, S.A. 78
Mollon, P. xv, 70, 90
moral defence 80
Morris, M. 88
mothers: depressed (2 case studies) 4–5, 29–30; drug addicted (case study) 74–75; intrusive versus withdrawn xvi, 16, 18, 41, 43, 73, 82–83; obsessive-compulsive (case study) 76–77, 103; relationship between infants and 50, 70, 72
mourning in therapy 96, 100

narratives, creating coherent xvi, 24, 25, 33, 96, 99–100; *see also* Lucy
neglect: consequences of xiii, 3–4, 8, 9, 18; in early childhood 10, 39, 41; *see also* Troy; Wes
"no-entry" defence 76–77, 83
normopaths 8
normotic patients 7

obsessive-compulsive behaviour 42, 76, 79
Oedipal relationships 30
offenders and dismissive attachment styles 87–88
Ogden, T.H. 8
Oliver (adult, punitive superego) 75–76, 77–78, 79, 83, 101
online counselling 91

parenting and avoidant personalities 53, 55
parents *see* children; mothers
Parker, M. 88
physical appearance as defence 81–82
"poisonous pedagogues" 71–72
preoccupied (enmeshed) personalities: characteristics and expectations xiii, 26, 38, 57; childhood development 85, 89; in couples 1–2, 45, 48, 51, 52, 53–55; in therapy 46, 59, 60–61, 62, 92; *see also* Sam and Gina

"psychic skin" defence xv–xvi, 86, 92
psychodynamic insights 24, 29–30, 48, 54
psychotherapy *see* therapy
punishment, corporal 71
pursuer/pursued relationships: dynamics of xv, 55, 55–57; therapy with couples in 62–63

questions, use in therapy 61–63

reciprocity xv, 9–10, 38, 46, 51
reflection/reflective functioning 3, 24, 46, 98, 99–100
Reibstein, J. 47
rejection: fear of 26, 27, 28, 41, 79, 81, 82; from caregivers 1, 39, 72, 73, 85, 89
Renn, P. 87
repression/inhibition as defence 70, 71, 87, 99; *see also* Oliver
research tools, attachment-based xiv, 24–28, 29, 31–33
"rhinoceros hide" defence xv–xvi, 86, 92
Rholes, W.S. 53
ritualistic behaviour as defence 79
Rosenfeld, H.A. 1

sadomasochism 81, 90, 101
Sam and Gina (avoidant/preoccupied couple) 55–56, 62–63
Schore, A.N. 18, 102
Scrooge, Ebenezer, archetypical avoidant character 105
secondary defences 85–86
secure attachment: characteristics of 26, 27, 96, 98–99, 100; conditions for developing 9–10, 89; in couple relationships 45, 46, 47, 48, 51
self-denial as defence 80–81, 83
self-harm 28, 29–30, 33, 89, 100–101; *see also* Lucy; Wes
self-punishment 81, 89, 100, 101
self-sufficiency: as characteristic of avoidant attachment 26, 27, 28, 32, 81, 86; children learning avoidance and 15, 16, 38, 73, 89; in couple relationships 48, 64; and culture 44; therapy and asking for help xii–xiii, 1, 91, 98

sex and avoidance 42, 46, 52, 53–54
shame: developing xv, 71–72, 77–78, 80, 82, 90; and therapy 97; *see also* Oliver
Slade, A. 99
social media, relating through xvi, 44–45, 52, 54, 84–85, 91
Solomon, M. 49
Spencer, H. 70
"stiff upper lip" personality style xiv, 2, 99
Strange Situation test 16, 71, 72
suicide *see* self-harm
super-ego, punitive 76, 80, 101, 102
systemic questioning in therapy 61–63

Target, M. 88, 99
Tatkin, S. 38, 45, 49, 60
technology, relating through xvi, 44–45, 52, 54, 84–85, 91
therapeutic boundaries 92–93, 96, 98, 104
therapists: personal attachment style 59, 104–105; personal background 44
therapy: aims and goals xvi, 26, 78, 95–97; challenges in working with avoidant adults xiii, 31–32, 42, 57–59, 64, 90; challenges in working with avoidant children 2–4, 8, 9, 18–19; clients' attitudes to xii, 90–92; clients' presentation in 92–95; with couples 46, 54–56, 59–63; focus areas in 97–103; use of research tools in xiv, 29, 33
Tommy (abused child) and countertransference 3–4

transference 9, 31, 44, 58, 93, 97
trauma, unresolved *see* Wes
Trevarthen, C. 10
Troy (overlooked child) 4–7
trust *see* mistrust/trust
Turkle, S. 85
Turp, M. 86

unconscious: importance in attachment-based therapy 25, 28, 63; role in couple relationships 50, 51, 53

violence and dismissing attachment styles 51, 87–88

Wallin, D.J. 39, 42, 58
Weeks, G. 59
Wes (adult, dismissive avoidant, unresolved trauma) 74–75, 77–78, 86–89
Weston, D.R. 72
Williams, G. 83
Winnicott, D.W.: on therapy 3, 41, 43, 64, 70, 94; *see also* Anna
withdrawn insecure styles: characteristics of 26, 27, 33; in couples under stress 40, 46, 47, 51; in therapy 60, 61, 62–63; *see also* Anna
withdrawn/intrusive mothers xvi, 16, 18, 41, 43, 73, 82–83
workaholism as defence 78–79

Zeifman, D. 50

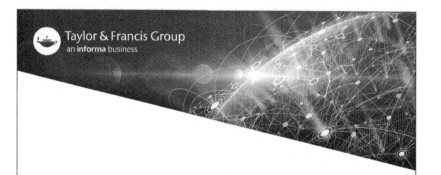

Made in United States
North Haven, CT
05 March 2023